PRAISE FOR MY *FAME, HIS FAME*

"In an age of platform building and fixation on building one's own personal 'brand,' Thann has given us a refreshing, much needed perspective regarding whose fame we ought to amplify. For it is from, to, and through Jesus Christ alone that are all things. I hope this book gains an audience with leaders especially. May we become larger by becoming smaller in our own eyes, and may we know true exaltation as we humble ourselves in the sight of the Lord, for the advancement of His fame and not our own."

—SCOTT SAULS, SENIOR PASTOR OF CHRIST PRESBYTERIAN CHURCH, NASHVILLE, TENNESSEE; AUTHOR OF *JESUS OUTSIDE THE LINES* AND *A GENTLE ANSWER*

"We live in a culture obsessed with personal fame—an idol that kills our faith and quenches the potential for miracles in our midst. Jesus said so Himself: 'No wonder you can't believe. For you gladly honor each other, but you don't care about the honor that comes from the One who alone is God' (John 5:44). If we ever needed to see God's intervention and to experience His miracle-working power, it's now. My friend Thann Bennett has written a passionate, powerful appeal to God's people. It's time to wake up, consecrate your life, and call on the name of the Lord. This book made me want to stand up and shout, bow low and pray, and believe that God will make Himself known in our day. Don't miss this timely word."

—SUSIE LARSON, NATIONAL SPEAKER, TALK RADIO HOST, AUTHOR OF *FULLY ALIVE*

"*My Fame, His Fame* is a wake-up call for Christians, to those of us seeking to know the face of Jesus. It is an invitation to look over into eternity and to call that vision into ou⸻ ⸻nd now."

—CASEY DIAZ, BESTSELL⸻ ⸻⸻⸻

"Few people do I trust more to discern the Father's voice than Thann Bennett. If your chief aim, like his, is to honor God with your life, this book shows you how—brilliantly and plainly explaining what gives our lives lasting, eternal significance: pursuing, partnering with, and pointing to God and His great fame!"

—JOHN JESSUP, CBN NEWS

"In a time when platform or influence is an ever-beckoning temptation, this book is a timely reminder about the one name we are supposed to make great. Through Thann's words, you will be inspired to proclaim the Lord in new and bold ways! What a privilege we have to make His name famous!"

—JOEL AND NINA SCHMIDGALL, AUTHORS OF
PRAYING CIRCLES AROUND YOUR MARRIAGE

"In a world where making a name for yourself is a common practice and expectation, *My Fame, His Fame* is a reminder to the believer that our pursuit is not about making our names famous. Thann shows us, through the life of Habakkuk, that humility in spirit and boldness of faith allows God's power and might to be on full display in our lives."

—JOSHUA SYMONETTE, TEACHING PASTOR AT NATIONAL COMMUNITY
CHURCH; FOUNDER OF BLU_PRINT, BALTIMORE, MARYLAND

"In a culture that seeks two minutes of fame, Thann calls us to something more noble and lasting: a lifetime of making the name of Jesus famous. With a mix of unique biblical study, practical theology, and engaging personal storytelling, *My Fame, His Fame* gives us permission to be drawn to fame and a blueprint for intertwining our everyday obedience with God's eternal glory. Bonus: it will make you an expert in the Old Testament prophet Habakkuk."

—HEATHER ZEMPEL, DISCIPLESHIP PASTOR AT NATIONAL
COMMUNITY CHURCH; AUTHOR OF COMMUNITY
IS MESSY AND AMAZED AND CONFUSED

MY
FAME
HIS
FAME

MY
FAME
HIS
FAME

AIMING YOUR LIFE
AND INFLUENCE TOWARD
THE GLORY OF GOD

THANN BENNETT

EMANATE
BOOKS

Published in Nashville, Tennessee, by Emanate Books, an imprint of Thomas Nelson. Emanate Books and Thomas Nelson are registered trademarks of HarperCollins Christian Publishing, Inc.

Thomas Nelson titles may be purchased in bulk for educational, business, fund-raising, or sales promotional use. For information, please e-mail SpecialMarkets@ThomasNelson.com.

Unless otherwise noted, Scripture quotations are taken from the Holy Bible, New International Version®, NIV®. Copyright © 1973, 1978, 1984, 2011 by Biblica, Inc.® Used by permission of Zondervan. All rights reserved worldwide. www.Zondervan. com. The "NIV" and "New International Version" are trademarks registered in the United States Patent and Trademark Office by Biblica, Inc.®

Scripture quotations marked KJV are from the King James Version. Public domain.

Scripture quotations marked THE MESSAGE are from *The Message*. Copyright © by Eugene H. Peterson 1993, 1994, 1995, 1996, 2000, 2001, 2002. Used by permission of NavPress. All rights reserved. Represented by Tyndale House Publishers, Inc.

Any Internet addresses, phone numbers, or company or product information printed in this book are offered as a resource and are not intended in any way to be or to imply an endorsement by Thomas Nelson, nor does Thomas Nelson vouch for the existence, content, or services of these sites, phone numbers, companies, or products beyond the life of this book.

ISBN 978-0-7852-3178-3 (eBook)
ISBN 978-0-7852-3177-6 (TP)

Library of Congress Control Number: 2019955992

Printed in the United States of America

20 21 22 23 24   LSC   10 9 8 7 6 5 4 3 2 1

May these pages channel the boundless Word of God, making their reach limitless and timeless, according to 2 Timothy 2:9.

For my brother Isaac, without whose encouragement I might never have written.

And for our parents: Dad and Mom Bennett, and Dad and Mom Gambrell, for giving us a heritage that speaks of His fame.

LORD, I have heard of your fame;
I stand in awe of your deeds, LORD.
Repeat them in our day,
in our time make them known;
in wrath remember mercy.

—HABAKKUK 3:2

CONTENTS

CONTENTS

FOREWORD

So far, so God" and "The best is yet to come."
These two statements are embedded in the DNA of our church, National Community Church in Washington, DC. For nearly twenty-five years, we have experienced countless moments where His divine plan and power has made a way for us. This firsthand experience with the fame of God has conditioned us to acknowledge that our past was only possible because of God, and to lean into our future with a holy expectation that He will continue to show up and show off.

Nine years ago, my son Parker and I visited Machu Picchu and went paragliding into the Inca Valley. Our only real orientation was an instruction to "run as fast as you can off the cliff and then lift your legs." Given the element of uncertainty we felt, I did what any good father would do—I let Parker go first!

When it was my turn and I was running toward the cliff, I had one thought in my head, *This is crazy.* But after leaping off the cliff and getting swept up in an updraft, that thought became *This is awesome!* Granted, I lost my lunch seven times, so it was decidedly less awesome for my tandem partner behind me!

Even so, the memory of that day reminds me that if we aren't willing to put ourselves in crazy situations, we will never experience crazy, awesome moments.

In Joshua 3, the Israelites experienced a crazy, awesome miracle when they crossed the Jordan River on dry ground. Most of us remember the miracle. But how many of us remember the crazy obedience that preceded the miracle?

In verse 3, after God instructed the Levites to move ahead with the ark of the covenant, the people were told, "You are to move out from your positions and follow it."

We should always plan and work like it depends on us, but it is far more critical to recognize when it is time to step out from the familiar and follow a move of God.

In verse 4, the people are told, "You will not know which way to go, since you have never been this way before."

The temptation to stay where it is familiar can be so strong. But charting a new path is often required in order to inherit the new thing God is doing.

In verse 5, Joshua gives the key instruction to the people, "Consecrate yourselves, for tomorrow the Lord will do amazing things among you."

This is the critical moment. It is God's job to do crazy, awesome things, but it is our job to consecrate ourselves to Him. The consecration is what affords us the capacity to dream beyond our ability and our resources.

Do you know how God makes big people? He gives them big dreams. By definition, a God-sized dream is beyond your ability and beyond your resources. You can't do it. But your God can! And when He does, He gets the glory. Show me your dream, and I will show you the size of your God.

In order for the people to experience the miracle of walking through the Jordan River, the people had to consecrate themselves, and the Levites leading them had to be willing to step into the river and get their shoes wet. They had to step out and follow a crazy instruction in order for the crazy, awesome miracle to occur.

God uses ordinary people who are consecrated to Him to do His most important work. He uses people who are willing to believe that if we do what God asks, He will reveal His fame of old in our day.

Like Thann, I believe God is preparing to do a crazy, awesome work in and through you. But I know from experience it will require you to step out and follow when He moves.

Would you be bold enough to believe with me that the best is yet to come?

Would you be audacious enough to get your shoes wet when He asks you to step into the river?

Our God is preparing to accomplish His will. He can do immeasurably more than we can ask or imagine. But He is asking you and me to be the catalysts for His mighty move. He has called us for such as a time as this—and for the purpose of calling His fame into our day. The only ceiling on what He is about to do is our level of consecration to Him.

Are you ready to step forward and consecrate yourself for the purpose of His fame? If so, buckle in and read on, because for those who are consecrated, the best is yet to come!

Mark Batterson
New York Times bestselling author of *The Circle Maker*
Lead Pastor of National Community Church

INTRODUCTION

· · · · ·

FAME

Look at the nations and watch—
and be utterly amazed.
For I am going to do something in your days
that you would not believe
even if you were told.
—HABAKKUK 1:5

I am terrified.

I am terrified I, despite having an intimate knowledge of the King of kings and the Creator of the universe, might never fully experience the awesome power of my God. I am terrified I might never yield fully to Him in a way that allows His intentions of glory revealed to occur through me. I am terrified the fame of my God might never be truly known in these times. In my time. And even if His fame and glory are revealed, I am terrified I might miss the role I am intended to play in bringing that dream into reality. I am troubled to think I might not get a chance to play the part He long ago created for me in making His fame known in my days.

So yes, I am terrified. And you should be similarly terrified.

But those shivers of terror are nothing compared to the shivers of exhilaration at the thought that my God might indeed be made known in my time. Those shivers intensify when I consider His fame might be realized anew specifically because of what He wants to do through me—the way He wants to tell His story through my story. To be sure, it would be enough for His fame to simply be made known in my time, no matter the vessel. That alone is the goal. But to be invited into that revelation, and to be entrusted with helping usher it in, is something infinitely beyond anything I could ask or imagine.

And yet, that is precisely my mission. It is exactly and without mistake my calling because I know of His power and His fame. I have heard of His mighty deeds. And I have the overwhelming good fortune of being invited to make that fame known in these times. In my time.

So I shiver with anticipation in a way that completely overwhelms my shivers of terror. You should shiver too. Because this is not my call alone. It is yours, as well. We are called to rise together as one with a single and unified mission in mind—that of making the Famous One known in our time. You, also, have heard of His mighty works and know of His power and fame. You, too, are called to usher in that fame in our time.

There was another who was terrified by these thoughts.

Another who shivered with terror but also with excitement and anticipation at the prospect of ushering in the fame of his God in his day and time. Another who longed for a revelation of the almighty God's fame but lost faith that it would occur on his watch. This one who shivered long before you and me was a prophet. This is his story.

THE PROPHET

The prophet had all but given up on God. He lived in times of great anguish and great oppression. The enemies of his people were terrorizing the land, and most around him were literally and figuratively on the run. It appeared God had abandoned them. It appeared their destruction was imminent and that God had turned His back. Time was running out, and the prophet's patience was running thin.

His patience was thin, his frustrations were high, and his hope was nearly gone. So he did the unthinkable. He confronted his God and placed the blame for his people's predicament squarely upon the almighty God.

The prophet told God he was tired of crying out for help, only to be ignored.

He accused God of not listening to his many pleas.

He blamed God for the violence the people were suffering, because God had not saved them.

He vented at God for tolerating what was happening and for forcing him to witness such atrocities.

He bemoaned that justice was yielding to injustice and that the law was being flouted with no consequence.

He informed God that the wicked were prevailing over the righteous, and he blamed his God for it.

Yes, the prophet was so desperate, times were so bad, and hope had run so thin, he turned on his God. He confronted his God with the brutal reality of the situation and asked why God had turned His back. It was not a prophet-like thing to do. Prophets are supposed to endure to the end. Prophets are supposed to weather the storms of life. When everyone else fades away and gives in to the troubles of the world around them, prophets are supposed to stand by their God.

Or are they?

What if a true prophet—a true follower of the King—is not designed to stand by while all around them falls but instead is created to be the one who walks into the storm to engage—and yes, even confront—the almighty God? What if the One who created us is not unaware of the storm that surrounds us but rather is desperately searching for someone who will finally run to Him with these many burdens and invite His mighty power to intervene in them? What if He is willing to be confronted by someone He created? What if the main purpose for the people He created is His interaction with them and through them in order to bring glory and fame to His name? What if a conduit for His glory and fame is what He has been seeking all along? What if He has stayed His hand simply because none of His creation has come to Him offering to be used by Him in this way?

What if we have had it all wrong? Because doesn't the prophet's situation feel a bit like today? Doesn't it feel as though the wicked are winning? Doesn't it feel as though the pleas of the righteous are being ignored? Doesn't it feel as if millions are suffering injustice and the justice of God is all too often absent? Doesn't it feel like your cries for solutions are being shouted into the void?

That is how it feels to me. And for so long, I have believed it inappropriate for me to say so out loud. After all, how dare I question God's timing or God's presence! He is all-knowing and all-powerful (both certainly true), and I have waited for Him to intervene in the situations around me. I have waited because I know He is already aware. I have waited because I know His power is sufficient. I have waited, and I have grown frustrated by the silence.

But maybe, just maybe, it is time for you and for me to follow the example of the prophet. Maybe it is time to confront the almighty God. Maybe He is just waiting for us to finally turn to Him. And maybe the reason He is waiting is because all of creation was intended to proclaim His fame, and He has stayed His hand until such a time that His fame could be revealed through our request and engagement.

Listen to the almighty God's response to the prophet's accusations: "Look at the nations and watch—and be utterly amazed. For I am going to do something in your days that you would not believe, even if you were told" (Hab. 1:5).

I am ready for that. I am ready for the God of the universe to step in and do something beyond my wildest imagination. I am ready for His time of silence to end and for wrongs to be made right. I am ready for His fame to roll through the land. I am ready for these days—my days, our days—to be marked by a move of the almighty God so great it has to be seen in order to be believed. And I am willing to be the one who confronts the almighty God for that purpose. I want nothing more than to give my life as a vessel through which the fame of my Creator can be made known. It is my greatest desire.

What about you? Are you also willing and ready?

THE PROPHET RESPONDS

The prophet was willing, and he demonstrated that willingness by confronting God. But even when God promised to move in a mighty way, the prophet was not convinced. He had been through too much and had witnessed a magnitude of injustice so great, he was rendered incapable of total belief without sight. And so he again reminded the almighty God of the turmoil the people were enduring while God stayed His hand. He asked, "Why are you silent while the wicked swallow up those more righteous than themselves?" (Hab. 1:13).

I have been there. In fact, I think I am there now. I know the power of the almighty God dwarfs these injustices I see, but they still loom so large compared to my own humanity. They loom large when the hand of God is stayed—when His fame is absent. They are small to Him, but they are overwhelmingly large to me.

It is time for Him to move.

It is time for Him to act.

I am stunned by the prophet's response. From this place of willingness riddled with doubt, the prophet tells the almighty God, "I will stand at my watch and station myself on the ramparts. I will look to see what he will say to me, and what answer I am to give to this complaint" (Hab. 2:1).

"I will stand at my watch and station myself on the ramparts." Though the prophet was unconvinced and though he had serious doubts, the prophet made a choice to take his place in the line of duty and stand watch in case the almighty God decided to move. The prophet was not yet convinced, but he moved into action. He was not sure when, or even if, God would meet him. But he vowed that if God did move, he would be found present on his watch and ready to join in that move.

Are you ready? Are you stationed at your watch? Are you guarding the ramparts? Or have you decided the almighty God is not true to His word and that He is not coming? Have you decided that if He is not showing up, neither will you?

It is time for all of us to step to our watch positions and eagerly expect a move of God. When the prophet made this move, God responded, "Write down the revelation and make it plain on tablets so that a herald may run with it" (Hab. 2:2).

God did in fact meet the prophet on the ramparts, but even then it was with a warning of more calamity to come. His instruction for the prophet was to make a proclamation of the looming destruction. A proclamation made from within the midst of the trial and storm. The prophet's task was to act in faith yet again and speak the fame of his God before that fame was present or evident. The prophet's proclamation would go before the fame and would actually usher in the fame. But in order for it to occur, the prophet had to be willing to utter it. He had to be willing to proclaim into the void.

Our task is the same. If we truly want to experience the mighty fame of our God in these times, we have to proclaim it. And we must do it into the void. We must do it before there is evidence of it. We must proclaim the fame of our God by faith and do it in the face of looming calamity. If we do not, His fame will remain veiled and His hand will remain stayed. But if we proclaim it, He has promised to do something in our time we would not believe even if we were told.

It is our move.

THE PROCLAMATION

Lord, I have heard of your fame.
—HABAKKUK 3:2

The prophet's proclamation—once he was finally convinced to make it—begins with a wistful recollection of the mighty acts of old. It is at once a statement of the almighty God's majestic power and an admission that the prophet has only secondhand knowledge of it. The prophet has only heard of God's great fame; He has never actually known it. The legends of God's mighty acts that are so needed in his present time are familiar to him, but only as a result of hearsay and legend. They remain something the prophet has heard about rather than something he has experienced.

So when the prophet is called to help usher in the fame of the almighty God, he has to resort to a declaration of faith about what he has heard from generations past. When the prophet opens his mouth to speak, it is not because his mouth is full of words describing what he has seen God do. No, quite the contrary! Remember, the prophet believes his God has been absent during his time. So the prophet opens his mouth in faith and begins with the best articulation of God's fame he knows. He begins with a recitation of the stories he has been told by those who have gone before him.

Maybe you feel as though you do not have your own stories of God's fame to tell. Maybe you are frustrated because you desire to speak of God's fame but have not felt His fame move on your behalf. That is how the prophet felt.

But I am willing to wager you have heard stories about God's goodness. You have heard legends about His great power. You have been told of His mighty hand moving on behalf of His people. In short, you have heard of God's fame.

Begin there. Tell those old stories of His power and might! I know it sounds extraordinarily simple—too simple in many ways—but our marching orders start with an instruction to simply proclaim that which we have been told about the fame of our God. The way we first step to our watch on the ramparts is by speaking in faith the fame of our God that is still secondhand to us. His desire is to reveal His fame firsthand—directly to us and for the benefit of our time. But that begins the same way it began for the prophet. It begins when we demonstrate faith in that which we have heard about the fame of our God.

"I have heard of your fame."

Are you ready to proclaim it?

THE LEGEND

The prophet proclaimed the fame of his God because he had heard the stories of old. Though he had not personally experienced the mighty acts of God, he knew of the legend.

What if I do not know the legend? What if I have not been imparted the stories and the wonders of God's power displayed to generations past? What if His majesty and greatness are not a tradition for my family name? What if I lack both the presence of God's fame *and* a personal knowledge of His legend? What then? Where do I turn to begin to understand how to walk in His power?

The journey to an answer for these questions begins when we muster the courage to venture into the unknown vastness of God. Our association with the legend grows as we acquire greater understanding that His power both fills the heavens and stoops to reach the lowly. It is more firmly grasped when we embrace the truth that our own understanding falls short, but His wisdom is fully sufficient and available to us. It is strengthened when we understand that our heritage—both the good and the bad—is part of our call. And it is more thoroughly realized when we recognize that we need His grace to cover our weakness.

The prophet knew the legend. But legends are not simply a birthright. They are not obtained only by inheritance. Legends can be learned. If you do not know God's fame through experience or inheritance, it is time to learn the legend. If you know His fame but the memory of its richness and power is faint, it is time to revisit it.

THE KNOWLEDGE

"I stand in awe of your deeds, Lord."

The prophet has not witnessed the fame of God, but he has heard of it, and now he has spoken of it. But it is one thing to speak with your mouth and another entirely to believe in your heart. We know from the holy Scriptures that both of these are required to receive the salvation of God (Rom. 10:9). We see from the prophet's example that both are also required if we are to experience a greater revelation of God's fame. The prophet did not just hear and proclaim. The prophet believed! How do I know? Because we do not stand in awe of things we do not believe. We are not moved to action by things we think are mere figments of our imaginations. No, we are moved to awe and action by things of which we have become convinced. By things that have ceased to be stories and legends and instead are rooted in what we know to be true!

Are you convinced? Are you convinced in your heart about the great fame of your God? Are you convinced that nothing in the universe—including great calamity and adversity—can separate you from His great love (Rom. 8:38–39)? Are you so convinced that it causes you to stand in awe of the deeds of your God that you have not yet personally witnessed?

If you and I want to see God's fame, we must move to a place of knowledge. We must stand in awe. If we want the impact of our lives and influence to be the furtherance of His name and fame, we must believe.

Do you believe?

Do you stand in awe?

THE REQUEST

"Repeat them in our day, in our time make them known; in wrath remember mercy."

The prophet has stepped to his watch. He has proclaimed that which he has heard. And he has become convinced that the legend of his God is true. But now it is time to call on the almighty God to come through. Now it is time to beckon those mighty acts of old into the present day. Now it is time for the prophet to move from "I believe my God can do it" to "Do it again, God!"

My friends, I believe we stand at a similar moment in history—both individually and collectively. I believe we are at a juncture where we desperately need God's fame to roll through the land. We desperately need our depravity and chaos to be met by the holiness, order, and power of our God. We need His fame and His glory to be repeated in our day, and in our time.

Do it again, God!

Are you courageous enough to ask it of Him? Are you bold enough to be the one who calls down His mighty power and lives a life dedicated to a greater revelation of His fame? Are you that convinced?

Candidly, while this is an exhilarating prospect, it is also an intimidating one. It is intimidating because the power of the almighty God is overwhelming, and many will greet it with skepticism and disbelief. If we dare place ourselves in association with His fame—and if, in fact, we are the ones who actually call that fame further into the open—it will cost us something. The price will vary, but each of us who makes this choice will pay a price. For some, it will be a reputational cost. For others, occupational. For others still, financial. And in truth, each of us must be prepared to give our very life for it.

The costs are many and at times high, but the payoff is something beyond our wildest imaginations. The payoff is God doing something we would not believe even if we had been told. The payoff is a repeat of the mighty acts of old. And it is a reorientation of our life's purpose toward the fame of our God.

Are you living with the aim of increasing the fame of your God? Does that aim supplant every other aim, including your own fame? Will you be satisfied if you hit the target and the result is that your fame is less but His is greater? If we can honestly answer yes, then I firmly believe it will usher in a mighty move of God, and we will begin to see His fame made known in our time.

Repeat your fame in our time, God. Do it again!

HABAKKUK

The prophet in this story is Habakkuk. But the call to him is now my call. It is now your call. The goal is for the fame of the almighty God to be revealed. The hope is to realize that dream in our time. The task is aiming the trajectory and influence of our lives in the direction of His glory. And the time is now.

Will you step to your watch? Will you station yourself on the ramparts in order to be ready when His fame rolls through the land? He is coming. He has said He is going to do something beyond anything we have ever experienced. Something beyond even those mighty acts of old. But whether or not we participate is up to us.

It is time to proclaim His fame. It is time to call down His mighty acts of old and see them repeated in our day. It is time to be a vessel for His mercy.

Are you in?

PART I

· · · ·

THE PROCLAMATION

Lord, I have heard of your fame.
—HABAKKUK 3:2

CHAPTER 1

· · · ·

FAMOUS

"I will make your name great."

—GENESIS 12:2

I won't be happy until I am famous like God."[1] Those are the words of the mega-superstar Madonna. They were not uttered at the beginning of her career or even as her fame was beginning to increase. They were spoken after she had accumulated about as much fame and adoration as is possible for a person. Madonna's goal was fame, and she had achieved it so fully that she was quite possibly the most famous woman on the planet. Yet it was still not enough.

This perspective is far from rare among the famous. In fact, I think it is fair to call it the norm. Most who have achieved a large dose of the fame they are pursuing will tell you it is not all it is cracked up to be. They will tell you it is not enough and that it is not a source of joy in the end. If that is true, then why are we still so drawn to fame? If those who have it tell us it does not satisfy, why do we still want it?

Would it shock you if I told you we are drawn to fame because we were created for it? It is true. We were created for fame, but somewhere along the way—somewhere right near the beginning—we lost sight of true fame. We confused the fame we were created for with the fame that can be gathered unto ourselves. We confused the fame our souls long for with the one our human flesh craves.

This human fame—rooted in a pursuit of "public estimation" or "popular acclaim"[2]—is an idea that consumes many of us in one form or another. We are a society thoroughly absorbed in the idea of persona. Platforms, likes, and influence are accepted measures of success. We live for the sound of applause and the adoration of the crowd. We pursue many things, but dare I say nothing with as much vigor as the allure of personal fame. We hear the words of the famous telling us that this fame is not the answer, and yet it still draws us.

The truth is, we are all drawn to this fame on some level. I use inclusive terms like "we" and "us" to describe this attraction because I know its pull in a personal way. I, too, feel the need to convince the world of my own value. I feel the urge to build up an image of myself that will impress the masses. The attraction to fame lives in me.

This attraction to fame exists across all personality types and on all points of the extrovert/introvert spectrum. Many of us crave the spotlight. Others prefer to be behind the scenes. These personality distinctions are not the point of contention. There is nothing inherently wrong with the spotlight, and there is no certain safety from the dangerous attraction of personal fame if we stay behind the scenes. Our disposition to the spotlight may differ, but the truth is, we are all drawn to this idea of fame.

Again, this may shock you, but I suggest the reason for the universal pull toward fame is that it is born at the soul level. I suggest we were actually made for fame, but it is a different kind of fame than we know and have been taught. It is a different kind of fame than the one that bombards us every day. It is a different fame, and it is a much, much greater fame.

It is a fame so great that each of us was birthed with a God-given desire for it. We were created to search out this fame, to amass it, to amplify it, and to give our lives for it.

It is true: this fame for which we were created is different from being famous. Some of our personalities are not inclined to become famous, but each of us is bestowed with a desire for fame—even if we do not yet realize it or possess an ability to articulate it. Our very design is intended to be inclined toward fame. We were created to pursue fame, to possess fame, and to channel fame. I would go so far as to suggest that the pursuit of this great fame should consume all the days of our lives.

We were made for fame.

But we so regularly confuse this fame we were created to pursue and possess with the allure of actually being famous. We confuse the two because the latter is the one we know and the one we see on display in the world around us. It is the one those around us are pursuing, and the one our world deems valuable. We are drawn to fame by our very nature, but we have fleshly tendencies that make us vulnerable to the fame our society holds in high regard. These two conceptions of fame are not only separate but are actually in conflict with each other.

If we are going to walk in the fame for which we were created, it will require that we learn to distinguish between His fame and the fame of this world.

CREATED FOR FAME

I am not famous and have no desire to become famous. But that is merely a personality preference. That is simply an indication of where I am naturally the most comfortable. It does not alter the fact that I, like Habakkuk, have heard of the almighty God's fame and have some semblance of a realization that my purpose for walking this planet is to build that fame. I am charged with cultivating that fame. I am tasked with proclaiming that fame. I am commissioned to be a catalyst for that fame and to propel it throughout all the land.

So despite a personality preference for relative anonymity, I have come to realize that my life's purpose is fame. But if I am to achieve my life's purpose, I have to learn about *true* fame. I will need to unlearn the version of fame I know—the one that bombards me every day. I will need to unlearn it so that the proper version might take its place. You see, the version of fame I know will destroy me. But the kind I was created to pursue will lift me from my weakness, set my feet on the heights, and impact the world in ways I could not even imagine.

You, too, were created for fame. You were created to be a partner in greatness and a mouthpiece for power. You were given a deep longing for things that transcend this world and for a title of royalty. Yes, you have been called to fame. But, like me, you are not called to this kind of fame by the world. It is not the fame that surrounds us. It is a fame with the power to right every wrong and heal every wound. It is a fame that causes the righteous to celebrate and the wicked to tremble. It is a fame that neither you nor I can fully fathom.

That is the fame for which we were created.

But before we give our lives in pursuit of it, we must unlearn the fame we know—the fame that pursues us with dangerous intent. We must reject a pursuit of the fame that will not satisfy until we are like God and take up a pursuit of the fame that actually belongs to God.

We were created for fame but not our own. We were created for so much more. We were created for the fame the prophet recalled. We were created for the fame of the almighty God.

HIS FAME OVER MY PERSONALITY

My personality prefers solitude over attention. Tranquility over fanfare. Backstage over center stage. I strongly dislike the idea of being an overly public figure. But if I am not careful, that personality preference can be a dangerous impediment to the main mission of my life: lifting high the Famous One. It can be an impediment because proclaiming the fame of our great God often requires visibility. It requires a public profession or even a loud proclamation. For Habakkuk, the proclamation "I have heard of your fame" was the turning point when a feeling of despondency and desperation became one of action and power. It was the moment in which Habakkuk moved from confronting God and turned to face the world with a public proclamation of God's awesome power. It was a moment when pretense and anonymity had to be left behind in order to make a bold statement about his God.

For me, the preference for working behind the scenes as opposed to in the limelight is not about a fear of the front lines. In fact, I have never found the stereotypical pressure-packed moment to be overwhelming, and to a certain extent I enjoy the adrenaline rush of a high-stakes moment or encounter. But when I zoom out and think about my preferred state of being, I definitely prefer privacy, solitude, and serenity. I prefer helping someone else make an impact while staying mostly hidden in the background.

For whatever reason, God has not always allowed this preference to prevail. I do serve in many supportive roles, and I am certainly not famous. But it is far from rare for God to ask something visible—something public—from me. You are right now holding one such example. After all, if the idea of writing, publishing, and promoting a book does not run contrary to a preference for remaining behind the scenes, then nothing does. But over time, my conviction for making known the fame of my God has grown to overwhelm my preference for anonymity. I still do not desire great amounts of attention or fanfare. But I would give anything—including my personal preference for anonymity—to amplify the fame of my God.

It is hard to say whether Habakkuk preferred fame or obscurity, but either way, this proclamation of God's fame is the decisive moment when he realizes he has fully aired his grievances with God and it is time to step forward in boldness. It is the moment when he steps from behind the curtain and onto the main stage. It is the moment when any preference for anonymity and any shame of association with his God are left behind. It is a moment of no turning back. Come what may, he is choosing to be visible and to publicly proclaim his belief that God's word is true. Habakkuk is staking his reputation on the prospect that God will keep His promise and actually show up on the scene.

Maybe you desire to be famous. Maybe the bright lights of the stage or the screen or the athletic field appeal to you. There is nothing inherently wrong with that preference. In fact, it is pretty normal, and each of us has some iteration of that tendency. Believe me, if my baseball abilities had afforded me the opportunity to play shortstop or catcher for the Chicago Cubs, I would have happily set aside my preference for anonymity and embraced baseball stardom!

On the other hand, maybe you prefer to be behind the scenes. Maybe you dislike being the center of attention. Maybe you, like me, gather greater fulfillment from solving a problem in the background than you do performing in the limelight. Again, there is nothing inherently wrong with that disposition. In fact, God has designed us to fulfill His unique plans for us.

But to be honest, our personality preferences are somewhat beside the point and is too often used as an excuse for our failure to obey. The truth is that each of us is called to respond with essentially the same act of obedience. Whether we desire personal fame or prefer anonymity, we are each called to live for the glory of His name. We are called to a decision point when our personal fame will be set aside in exchange for a life devoted to proclaiming the fame of the Famous One.

"Lord, I have heard of your fame." Habakkuk's decision point came before He witnessed a move of God. In fact, God was waiting to move until Habakkuk would proclaim. He was waiting for Habakkuk to proclaim because He desired that Habakkuk be the vessel for His fame. This is what makes our proclamation of faith so tricky. If we are going trade the fame we know for the fame we were designed to carry, it will require a proclamation of faith. It will require that we step proactively onto the ramparts and believe that God will meet us there.

A proclamation of God's fame is the first step toward the goal of being a catalyst for His mighty works in our generation. In order to successfully navigate this transition, we must first grapple with this concept of personal fame. We must learn God's design for earning a reputation in all the land and leading lives focused solely on His fame.

A GREAT NAME

"I will make your name great."

Those six words were part of God's promise to the patriarch of the Old Testament, Abram, in Genesis 12:2. The promise was a precursor to Abram's name change to Abraham and to the emergence of a miraculous people through Abraham's lineage. It was a foretelling of something that seemed impossible at the time. But it was not aimed at something so small as one man's reputation or legacy. Rather, Abraham's name was to be made great in order to lay a foundation for the coming of the King. Abraham's greatness was merely a springboard for the true greatness that would follow.

This promise is similar in many ways to other foretelling promises in Scripture, particularly the promise made to the Israelites exiled in Babylon (Jeremiah 29). Just as many of us remember the "I will make your name great" part of Abram's promise, many of us know and hold to the beautiful promise in Jeremiah 29:11: "For I know the plans I have for you," declares the LORD, "plans to prosper you and not to harm you, plans to give you a hope and a future." We remember and claim these portions of the promises because it is easy to desire a great name and a condition of prosperity. But I suggest that sometimes a focus on these aspects of the promises actually causes us to miss the most powerful promises in the passages.

In both promises—to Abram and the exiled Israelites—there are two principles that we can expect in our lives, as well.

First, it is God—not us—who will make our names great and prosper us, and He will do it if it serves the purpose of making His name famous. In each of these promises, while we are tempted to hear mainly what is being promised to us, God is speaking primarily about what He will do ("I will make—" and, "I know the plans I have—") and how it will bring Him glory ("all the peoples on earth will be blessed through you," and "I will be found by you").

So first and foremost, this concept of fame is entirely for the purpose of amplifying God's name. To the extent we are afforded any portion of a certain fleeting type of fame, it both comes from God and is intended for God and His glory. It is meant to flow through us, not rest upon us.

Second, the process of knowing God's fame and walking in His promises can be a long and painful one. Abram and Sarai were already decades beyond childbearing years when this promise of a great family legacy was made to them. But even upon receipt of the promise, they were instructed to pack up their entire life and set out on a difficult journey to essentially start over (Gen. 12:1). The promise of God was not simply set in front of them. Instead, they were called to step forward and act out in obedience. They were called to proclaim and obey before they had evidence that God's promise was true.

In the case of the Israelites, the beautiful promise of prosperity is preceded by this often overlooked premise: "When seventy years are completed for Babylon, I will come to you and fulfill my good promise" (Jer. 29:10). Seventy years! Seventy years of exile, no less. Practically speaking, that meant most of the people receiving this beautiful promise would not live to walk in it. At the very least, it would be only the young who realized it first-hand, and they would be old before they did.

We need to come to terms with the reality that a pursuit of God's fame is not an overnight endeavor. It is not a scratch-off lottery ticket. Rather, it is a glimpse of the glory that God intends to do in and through us if we persevere. It is a merciful dose of what awaits us on the other side of our current suffering. Our God is telling us what He will do in order that we might muster the courage to do what is set before us.

Might I suggest that this reality makes the promises of God more attractive rather than less? It does so because it invites us to walk in a small portion of what He experienced for us on the cross. It enables us to know at least a sliver of how much He loves us—enough to pay everything in exchange for our redemption. Now, He offers us His shared glory. But if you are in a place of starting over, or if you have been exiled for a long time, take heart! Those are the places where we are emptied of ourselves in order to receive more of Him.

He has promised to give us each a great name. But we must grasp the reality that the world does not need our great names. We see a broken culture and we want to fix it. But we—and our own personal fame—are not the answer. The world does not need us. The world needs the Famous One. But God, in His infinite wisdom and desire for interaction with us, has intertwined our call with His fame. He has created us to be the way in which He reaches the world.

So while the world may not need us, we are the way in which it gets the One it needs. We are the way in which the world gets Him. It is through us that the Famous One is made known. He has called us to live a life dedicated to His fame, and in return He has promised us a great name. He has given us His assurance not that we will be famous but rather that our names will be hidden within His great fame.

Our task is to aim every influence of our lives in the direction of His fame.

CHAPTER 2

. . . .

KNOWN

But whoever loves God is known by God.

—1 CORINTHIANS 8:3

We try to be famous when we should long to be known. We strive to prove we know best when we should be seeking to be known by the One who knows all. We endeavor to make our names known when our only goal should be that we are fully known by Him. To put it plainly, it is far better to be known than it is to be famous.

We have established that we were created to pursue, possess, and even channel fame, but we have so frequently misallocated where that accumulated fame is to reside. There is an ever-present clash of ideals between what it means to be famous and what it means to be known. If we are to have any success in our pursuit of His fame, it will require that we reorient ourselves toward His design. He desires that we be fully known by and hidden in Him. He desires that we pursue knowledge of His face and a dedication to His fame. These two objectives go hand in hand and cannot be effectively achieved apart from each other.

This reorientation toward a focus on being truly known by Him begins with a commitment to vulnerability before Him. He wants to give us a great name and help us earn a reputation throughout the land, but it requires a life that is fully given over to Him. It does not require a perfect life—far from it! In fact, it is clear He has repeatedly chosen for His work those who have abandoned pretense in favor of an embrace of their own weakness. He is looking for those who would seek genuine, transparent relationship with Him—those who would lay down their own reputations in favor of His. In other words, He is looking for those who desire to be known in every way—failures and all.

This idea has become easier for me to grasp since becoming a father. When one of our children says something like "You are the best dad in the world," it absolutely melts my heart. It is the best affirmation they can give, and the weight of its value is increased by the fact that our relationship is genuine. My kids know all too well that I am not perfect, and they know I am aware of their imperfections as well. This mutual and genuine relationship makes an expression of great love all the more meaningful because it flows from a place of intimate knowledge of my shortcomings. It is truly unconditional.

I suggest it is not all that different for our heavenly Father. He wants to know every part of us and to express His unconditional love for us even while fully aware of our weakness. He is not looking for perfection, but He does desire full surrender. He longs to know us in full.

If we are to be used by Him in a way that proclaims His fame, we must set our hearts not on fame but on being *known* by the Famous One. We must lay down our reputation in exchange for His and trust that He will build for us a reputation capable of carrying His fame.

It is better to be known than to be famous.

FAME IN THE LAND

The battle of Jericho is probably the event for which the biblical hero Joshua is best known. Joshua followed God's instructions and defeated the fortified city of Jericho simply by having his people march around the walls for seven days and then raise a mighty shout. The walls of the city fell to the ground, and God delivered a great victory to the Israelites. It is an incredible story of God's power, but I am most intrigued by what followed this great victory.

After the walls fell, Joshua issued this stern warning against anyone who would seek to rebuild the destroyed city: "At the cost of his firstborn son he will lay its foundations; at the cost of his youngest he will set up its gates" (Josh. 6:26).

The very next verse, Joshua 6:27, says, "So the LORD was with Joshua, and his fame spread throughout the land."

Generally speaking, threatening to kill your people's children is a terrible strategy for achieving fame—at least the positive kind! But Joshua was not seeking fame; He was focused on obeying the voice of God and convincing his people to honor the command against rebuilding Jericho. As a result of his obedience, Joshua's reputation in the land was strengthened, and, more important, his association with the Famous One now went before him.

Just a few chapters later we find that the Gibeonites traveled to meet Joshua and deceived him into granting a promise of protection. Joshua's fame had gone before him to such an extent that the Gibeonites begged to become servants rather than be destroyed. To be honest, that does not sound like much of a step up to me, but they were successful in their deception and Joshua granted their request.

But notice the motivation behind their great effort to seek Joshua's favor. When Joshua asked who they were, the Gibeonites responded:

> Your servants have come from a very distant country because of the fame of the LORD your God. For we have heard reports of him: all that he did in Egypt, and all that he did to the two kings of the Amorites east of the Jordan—Sihon king of Heshbon, and Og king of Bashan, who reigned in Ashtaroth. (Josh. 9:9–10)

The Gibeonites were lying about where they came from (in truth, they were neighbors), but they were certainly not lying about why they knew Joshua's name! "Because of the fame of the Lord your God!" When was the last time someone showed up to see you unannounced because they knew you were associated with a God so powerful they simply had to be on good terms with you? Maybe it is a different answer for you, but for me the answer is never. I regularly have unscheduled meetings with people who want to accomplish a legislative goal or have a particular message to spread, but I have never—not once—had this Joshua moment where someone has heard about the fame of my God because of something I have done and then scrambled to meet me as a result.

In many ways I think it is an indictment of my own priorities. I should be desperate to make the fame of my God known in the land. Sometimes that requires our own association with Him to be boldly proclaimed or acted upon. Humility is a noble pursuit— maybe even our highest calling, but refusing to be widely seen in association with the almighty God is not humility. In fact, it is the exact opposite. It is prioritizing my comfort and personal preference over what should be the driving goal of my life: making known the name of the almighty God!

I do not want to be famous. But I desperately want to have a reputation in the land that facilitates the fame of my God.

A GLIMPSE OF GOD

As we become more fully known by God, our desire to know more of Him in return will naturally grow stronger. We see numerous biblical examples of this, and I have drawn strength from several contemporary examples as well.

On the biblical side of the equation, the story of Moses paints an epic picture of a very flawed man who was called by God to do great things, and who grew ever more fervent in his desire to know the face of God and to obey His voice. There is no illusion or suggestion that Moses succeeded effortlessly in this area. In fact, he specifically struggled with it. His anger at God, the people, or himself repeatedly presented a relational hurdle for Moses to clear. But God continued to pursue Moses, and Moses continually returned with even greater resolve to his pursuit of knowing the face of God.

My favorite illustration of Moses' desperation to know more of God occurs in Exodus 33, as Moses was pleading with God to reveal more of Himself in order to confirm the instructions He had given. Moses had been speaking with God "face to face, as one speaks to a friend" (v. 11). God told Moses, "I know you by name and you have found favor with me" (v. 12). Yet, despite this intimate knowledge of and relationship with each other, Moses had not seen God with his physical eyes, and he longed to do so. Moses pled that God's presence would go with him, and God granted the request specifically because Moses was known by God: "I will do the very thing you have asked, because I am pleased with you and I know you by name" (v. 17).

God said yes, but Moses was not satisfied. He wanted to *see* God. Moses responded, "Now show me your glory" (v. 18).

Sometimes we seek God's face and His intervention, but we walk away satisfied after receiving a narrow answer. Our thirst is quenched when God has addressed the situation at hand. We accept this narrow answer from God because we are still more concerned with our circumstances than we are our relationship with Him. But not Moses. Moses wanted to *see* God, and while he had God's attention, Moses insisted that God reveal a bit more of His glory.

God's response should make the hair on your neck stand up:

And the LORD said, "I will cause all my goodness to pass in front of you, and I will proclaim my name, the LORD, in your presence. I will have mercy on whom I will have mercy, and I will have compassion on whom I will have compassion. But,"

he said, "you cannot see my face, for no one may see me and
live." Then the LORD said, "There is a place near me where you
may stand on a rock. When my glory passes by, I will put you
in a cleft in the rock and cover you with my hand until I have
passed by. Then I will remove my hand and you will see my
back; but my face must not be seen." (Ex. 33:19–23)

When Moses insisted and persisted rather than relenting,
God granted his wish to observe a portion of the glory of God
with physical eyes. What a moment that must have been! What
a lesson about how God can handle a little stubborn persistence
from those of us who desire to know Him and be known by
Him. What an important reminder that God desires authentic
relationship with us above a pious reverence that prevents us
from pressing in to Him.

Also, what a staggering depiction of the vastness of God's
glory. Moses, one of the great heroes of faith in the Bible, must
be hidden in a rock and shielded by the hand of God in order to
be protected from being consumed by the full glory and fame
of God's presence. Even Moses was only permitted a glimpse of
God's greatness. Even he could only handle exposure to the back
side of God's fame.

Friends, the fame of our God is vast beyond our imaginations. Are we adequately desperate for even a glimpse of it? Do
we know what even the back side of that glory looks like? Are we
desperately seeking to be known by God in a way that allows us
a face-to-face audience with Him? Are we using that audience to
insist that God show us His glory?

He is willing to reveal His glory. He desires to know and
be known. But we have underestimated His vastness. We have

declined to insist on more of His glory. As a result, He has shielded us from a glimpse of His glory.

It is time for that to change.

God, show us Your glory!

THE FAR SIDE OF GOD

Once we have a glimpse of God, I am convinced it will fuel a passion for more of Him. Our worship pastor at National Community Church, Chris Douglas, and his wife, Kathryn, have been an example to Brooke and me in recent days of this transition. Chris and Kathryn recently walked through the unspeakable horror of losing a young child. Grief from burying their child left its mark on Chris and Kathryn, and our church family grieved with them. After a time of reflection and restoration, Chris has talked and written openly about what it is like to endure such a deep wound and about the effort it takes to keep hold of God's promises.

But I am most moved by Chris's description of the place they find themselves in on this side of their loss. He described it as being "unsatisfied with what we had previously known about God." He said, "I am no longer satisfied with knowing the near side of God. I am desperate to know the far side of God." What a powerful illustration of how a time when God feels distant can fuel our longing to know more of Him. Because when what we know of God does not feel sufficient for our current trials we have two choices: to walk away or to press in deeper until we find more of Him.

What will we do when what we know of God—our glimpse of God—does not feel like enough to sustain us? What will we do when the near side of God's glory is all we have? The vastness of God is unknowable and unattainable, but there is a far side of His character and His being that is knowable if we will press in rather than walk away.

I want to press in. I want more than just a glimpse of God. I want to be known by Him in a way that allows me to know the far side of His glory and fame. I want to know and be known in a way that allows me to truly insist that He move in my time.

God, give me more than just a glimpse of You! Show me the far side of Your glory!

WHERE AM I KNOWN?

Where am I known? Another way to ask it is, Where does my fame reside?

It is a critical question to answer honestly, because if I am best known by the Famous One, I will be most motivated by the things that proclaim His name. On the other hand, if I am best known by those around me, I will be most motivated by the things that preserve my fame in their eyes.

As with so many areas of life, this is ultimately a matter of the heart. It is a question of where we are laying up treasure and what truly drives us. It is a choice, because we can only serve one master (Matt. 6:24). It requires an understanding that we cannot effectively amplify His fame unless we are fully hidden in Him. Conversely, we cannot be hidden in Him unless His fame is our highest goal.

There is a sobering two-edged component to this concept. So far, we have focused mostly on the exhilarating possibilities that exist if we dedicate ourselves to God's fame and to being known by Him. But it is equally true that if we choose to devote ourselves to our own fame and our own reputation, those lesser desires will enslave us (Gal. 4:9.) If we become more concerned with whom God is using—and whether or not it is us—than we are with the simple desire that He move, we fall into this trap.

Numbers 12 gives us an example of this danger in the lives of Aaron and Miriam. God had been using Moses in ways that were nothing short of miraculous. God and Moses had been interacting face-to-face, and God's power had been consistently flowing through Moses on behalf of the Israelites. The people's very existence had been preserved because of God's power on display through Moses.

Even so, Aaron and Miriam responded with jealousy: "Has the LORD spoken only through Moses?" they asked. "Hasn't he also spoken through us?" (Num. 12:2). In other words, "Look at us! We are great too!"

It sounds like such a ridiculous and selfish exclamation when we read it, but I think many of us do this on a regular basis. We see a spark of God's glory at work, but our natural inclination is not one of considering how it can be fanned into full flame, but rather one of wondering how we can be cast favorably in its glow. We see God's fame as being for our glory rather than viewing our beings as vessels for His. We envy the Moses figures in our lives at this moment, and we justify it by saying that we also desire to speak with God face-to-face. But much like Aaron and Miriam, we are all too often motivated by a desire for the people to look at us instead of at God.

We also forget all that Moses sacrificed for this relationship with God, and we do the same with people of our generation. We forget that Moses continued to serve even though God barred him from entering the promised land (Num. 20:12). We forget that God had decided to abandon His people because of their stubbornness, and it was Moses who convinced God to be gracious and to remain with them (Ex. 33). It was Moses who had given everything so that his people might reap the rewards. And yet Aaron and Miriam thought they wanted what Moses had.

Living for God's fame can come at a heavy price. There is no guarantee we will reap the rewards on this side of eternity. In fact, it is very likely that God's moving through us will be the cause for those around us to resent us or abandon us. But keep your eyes fixed on His glory, because in the end you will reap just rewards.

Finally, let us all lay aside this foolish notion that we should be ungrateful for the roles God has assigned us. Instead, let us endeavor to unleash a move of God in our time, no matter the vessel. When He chooses to use us, let us step forward and run with it! When he chooses another, let us step behind them and support them with everything we have. It is all for His fame, anyway.

Where are you known?

Where does your fame reside?

Are you fully known by and hidden in Him?

When God moves through another, are you willing to fall in behind them?

Yes, we were made for fame—His fame. We obtain and amplify that fame when we are fully known by Him. It is better to be known than to be famous.

CHAPTER 3

FOLLOW THE LEADER

My soul followeth hard after thee;
Thy right hand upholdeth me.

—PSALM 63:8 KJV

I cringe just a bit whenever I hear the word *leadership*. I cringe not because I think it an unimportant concept or because I have not benefited from great leaders in my life. In fact, the exact opposite has been true. I have had and continue to have the tremendous privilege of serving alongside some of the great leaders of our time. Whatever growth has occurred in me over the years is due in large part to the exemplary leadership of those who have invested in me. Leadership skills are invaluable, and there are many terrific voices to foster and steward those skills. But

I cringe because all too often we are encouraged to pursue the wrong kind of leadership, and it is suggested to us that leadership should be one of the primary goals we pursue.

Time and time again we are called to push our way to the front and develop skills that will make people want to follow us. We are encouraged to hold our heads high, draw on our charisma, and outshine the competition to attract more followers and gain more influence. We are told that working to increase our fame is justified in this case because it is for the good purpose of reaching more people with the message of Jesus Christ.

Not everything about this model is incorrect, but it is built on a fatally flawed premise and is fraught with danger. The book of James warns us, "Not many of you should become teachers, my fellow believers, because you know that we who teach will be judged more strictly" (James 3:1). The danger is that if we are pursuing leadership for the sake of a larger audience, the only thing we are adding to our portfolios is personal responsibility and accountability for which we were not intended. If we pursue fame in ways God has not intended, or in a fashion or time He did not ordain, we are setting ourselves up for failure. Even worse, we are leading astray those who may follow.

God's design is just the opposite. His design is that we *follow* well. His charge is that we follow hard after Him. Ironically, the natural result of following hard after Him will often be magnetic, and in many cases people will naturally follow. But the goal must always be that they follow Him rather than us. Worthwhile leadership requires a focus not on who and how many are behind us but on who and how fervently we are following the One who goes before us. It is about setting our eyes ahead on the One we are following rather than behind on the ones who may be following us.

I so appreciate the way our worship leader at National Community Church, Nicois Harris, communicated this concept. She said, "Hearing His voice is so much more important than finding my voice." It is doubly ironic because hearing His voice is the only real way for Him to fill us with His voice as promised in Jeremiah 1:9: "Then the LORD reached out his hand and touched my mouth and said to me, 'I have put my words in your mouth.'" Hearing His voice is not only more important than finding my voice; it is also the way in which I find my voice in Him.

As we grapple with this idea of laying down our fame in favor of lifting high the Famous One, the concept of following hard may be the most important one to conquer in our lives. Please hear me—I am not condemning influence. In fact, this book recounts several examples of leaders whose fame is made known in all the land. But influence that is worth something beyond our own egos involves a perspective far different than a focus on how large or well-positioned we have built our platforms. True influence—and worthwhile leadership—is fixing our eyes on the One we are following rather than on those who may be coming behind.

True leadership is more about following hard than it is about how many are following us. It is about following the Leader more than it is about leading those who are following. It is less about our ability to impress and more about having the humility to submit. True leadership requires we become follower-leaders.

GETTING PASSED

True follower-leaders get passed. In fact, one of the best ways to determine whether you are walking in this kind of followership is to look around and see if any of those you have been "leading" are passing you. This does not always occur in a linear way or necessarily translate to human titles or prestige, but if you are truly following hard after Jesus, those who are attracted to follow in your wake should be passing you in some areas and in some instances. If we are faithfully modeling for others what it means to have eyes fixed on Him, we should be seeing them drawn deeper and deeper into His call for their lives as well.

In the typical leadership model, a leader seeks to acquire a larger audience and more influence over time and always in an upward direction. In God's design, a follower-leader's audience may ebb and flow over time as God uses that follower-leader in different ways or as a result of God doing a new work in that follower-leader. Similarly, while a traditional leader is constantly drawing others toward his or her influence, a follower-leader is incorporating the voice of other teachers and instructors who are also following hard after the Famous One.

Does this approach mean we will get passed more often? Yes! And we should revel in that reality. When a leader's reach is restricted to those within his or her influence, he or she is choosing to prioritize personal fame over the elevation of God's fame. Rather than aspiring to keep others safely in our wake, we should be fervent in our efforts to propel them onward and even ahead of us. Not only does this perspective shield us from accountability that God did not intend us to have, but it also multiplies the impact we can have on behalf of His fame.

If we want to truly know—and truly experience—the fame of God, we have to be willing to get passed by those we are leading.

HONE YOUR MESSAGE

I want to be careful to avoid any suggestion that this pursuit of becoming follower-leaders warrants a resting on our laurels. Because just as a pursuit of our own visibility is out of step with God's design, a refusal to hone our message and discipline our minds for the tasks He is preparing for us constitutes a squandering of His call for us.

First Peter 3:15 says it this way: "Always be prepared to give an answer to everyone who asks you to give the reason for the hope that you have."

Always be prepared. That does not happen by chance. Living prepared and ready to respond to an opportunity to proclaim God's fame is not simply a matter of the heart or a simple choice. Yes, our hearts must be in the proper posture. Yes, we must choose in advance that we will respond when an opportunity presents itself. And yes, God has promised to send His Holy Spirit to provide words in a moment of need (Luke 12:11–12). But none of that fully heeds the admonition that we "always be prepared to give an answer to anyone who asks you to give the reason for the hope that you have."

Preparation is hard work. Preparation takes time. Preparation means marinating in God's Word. It means deepening our mental and experiential interaction with His commands. And yes, it means honing our message. It means practicing and developing our delivery skills. It means sharpening the communication tools God has given us. It means anticipating that God will bring the opportunities and trusting that His Holy Spirit will lead in the moment, but also preparing ourselves—mind, body, and spirit—in order that we live always at the ready.

Choosing to be a follower-leader does *not* mean declining to prepare. Just the opposite! We are each called to hone our message and our communication skills in order that we might have maximum effectiveness when God calls our number.

FOLLOW THE FAME

These ideas of fame and following are intricately intertwined. In all reality they are impossible to properly develop apart from each other. The only way to be truly caught up in the stream of God's fame is to live fully within His shadow. Conversely, the only way to follow hard after Him is to be completely fixated on, and by, His fame and majesty. It is a yes-and equation rather than an either-or question.

The book of Job gives a good illustration of this reality. As Job went through dramatic peaks and valleys of life, his friends also went through wild swings of usefulness—sometimes offering wise counsel and sometimes kicking Job while he was down. In Job 5, Job's friend Eliphaz had been recounting some of Job's travails. But I love what Eliphaz said when he pivoted to giving Job advice on how to respond to those challenges. He said, "If I were in your shoes, I'd go straight to God, I'd throw myself on the mercy of God. After all, he's famous for great and unexpected acts" (Job 5:8–9 THE MESSAGE). The NIV translation says, "But if I were you, I would appeal to God; I would lay my cause before him. He performs wonders that cannot be fathomed, miracles that cannot be counted."

"If I were in your shoes, I'd go straight to God." Why? Because He is famous! Because He is powerful. Because He can deliver you.

We need His fame and His power, but in order to obtain it, we have to follow it. We cannot be afraid to associate with it. We have to prepare to walk in its stream. And when the moment comes—be it one of great opportunity or great adversity—we must be willing to follow the fame.

If I were you, I would run to God.

I would run to God because He is famous.

He is famous because He performs wonders that cannot be fathomed.

That is the God I would run to.

WHO CHARTS MY PATH?

You might be asking, *What does it really matter?* You might be thinking, *This theory about focusing on following rather than leading is fine, but it is just semantics and does not make much difference.* Those are fair questions and musings to have, and I confess to sharing them regularly. But a proper perspective on this dichotomy is in fact one that will make or break us. It is as crucial and foundational to the plan God has for us as anything outside of salvation.

The reason this concept is so critical is pretty straightforward. If we do not achieve a proper focus on following rather than leading, our choices will be dictated based on the anticipated response of our followers rather than on the plain commands of the One we are following.

It really boils down to the fact that we can only serve one master. Matthew 6:24 says, "No one can serve two masters. Either you will hate the one and love the other, or you will be devoted to the one and despise the other." We can reach and impact many realms and communities, but we can only have true fidelity to one. When the commands and teachings of the One conflict or discomfort the many who follow, which allegiance will we choose? When following hard and holding fast to Him means losing our grip on those within our influence, will we follow hard and hold fast anyway? Or will we slow our pursuit and relax our grip in order to accommodate those we don't want to lose as followers?

Even those who personally witnessed the ministry of Jesus struggled with this: "Yet at the same time many even among the leaders believed in him. But because of the Pharisees they would not openly acknowledge their faith for fear they would be put out of the synagogue; for they loved human praise more than praise from God" (John 12:42–43).

"They loved human praise more than praise from God." Even more astonishing, the main cause of their hesitancy to openly profess belief was a fear of being thrown out of the church. Many of the people believed, but their highest priority was still maintaining favor with those around them. They wanted to be liked and accepted. They wanted a relationship with Jesus to follow the path they had already charted rather than allow an authentic relationship with Him to chart a new path for their lives. They were still more focused on and concerned with the reaction of those around them than they were on following hard after the One who was calling them.

Even Pilate, when he was considering what to do with the accusations against Jesus, struggled with this choice. Pilate had found Jesus to be innocent, and yet he agreed to hand him over to a murderous, bloodthirsty mob in order to be crucified. Why would a person of rank, influence, and authority do such a vile thing? He did it because he was more interested in pleasing the people than he was in standing on the truth.

> "What shall I do, then, with the one you call the king of the Jews?" Pilate asked them.
> "Crucify him!" they shouted.
> "Why? What crime has he committed?" asked Pilate.
> But they shouted all the louder, "Crucify him!"
> Wanting to satisfy the crowd, Pilate released Barabbas to them. He had Jesus flogged, and handed him over to be crucified. (Mark 15:12–15)

"*Wanting to satisfy the crowd.*" Pilate, a leader of many, was not concerned about where he was leading the many but rather was consumed by the anticipated reaction of the many. Because of this addiction to appeasing the crowd, Pilate surrendered an innocent man to be slaughtered by the followers Pilate was desperate to keep.

Forgive me for being forward, but Pilate's approach strikes me as not that different from much of the leadership style we often pursue in our own lives. We spend an enormous amount of time trying to figure out what the people want. In the political world, it looks like polling and peer-group testing. In my life, it looks like an obsession to put forward an image that will be embraced by those I encounter. For all of us, it so often involves making choices not based on what will take us in the right direction but based on what will place us at the front of the crowd. We are less concerned about the direction the crowd is heading than we are about where we are positioned within the crowd.

This type of leadership is worse than worthless. It is highly destructive, and it results in us being responsible for furthering the lost state of those around us. It is tempting to buy into the notion that if we can just do what it takes to gain an audience with the lost, we can win them over for Him. The problem is that if we win influence with someone by virtue of pandering to their demands, we forfeit any ability to call them to a life that places their demands in a subservient position to the demands of the Famous One.

This is not an easy thing. Do not lose heart if this idea does not sit well with you. It does not naturally sit well with me, either. Our human nature is inclined to please people and to seek out favor from the world. Making a commitment to follow hard after Jesus in a way that will not always easily translate to those in our world is a difficult hurdle to clear. Paul, in his letter to the church in Galatia, put it this way: "Am I now trying to win the approval of human beings, or of God? Or am I trying to please people? If I were still trying to please people, I would not be a servant of Christ" (Gal. 1:10).

Friends, if our highest goal in life is to attract a crowd and accumulate followers, becoming a servant of Christ is not the way to accomplish it. If our primary aim is to please and appease those who might be looking to us, we are going to miss the mark. Worse yet, we will miss the mark on behalf of not only ourselves but also all of those we have attracted as a following. If we want to please people, there are many effective ways for doing so. If you choose to walk that path, many will affirm you as a great leader. But you will not be using the impact of your life to amplify the fame of your God.

The fame of your God will be lifted high when you choose to follow hard after Him.

The fame of your God will be lifted high when you choose to look for approval not to those who are following behind you but to the One you are following hard after.

The fame of your God will be lifted high when you lay down the pursuit of leadership in exchange for the incredible privilege, honor, and calling of following.

Let Him chart your path.

Choose to follow.

Follow hard.

CHAPTER 4

. . . .

LOOKING OVER

Since, then, you have been raised with
Christ, set your hearts on things above,
where Christ is, seated at the right hand of
God. Set your minds on things above, not
on earthly things. For you died, and your
life is now hidden with Christ in God.

—COLOSSIANS 3:1-3

On April 3, 1968, Martin Luther King Jr. delivered one of his most famous and enduring speeches. The setting was a rally of striking sanitation workers at Mason Temple in Memphis, Tennessee. The flashpoint that initiated the strike had occurred a couple of months before when two workers, Echol Cole and

Robert Walker, were killed on the job because of faulty equipment. While the death of these two men ignited the community and launched the strike, the truth is that the entire nation was already on the brink. Racial tension was simmering everywhere, but it was boiling faster in certain places all across the country—maybe nowhere more so than Memphis. The long-overdue movement for equality and civil rights was finally gaining traction, and the Memphis Sanitation Workers' Strike was viewed as a critical catalyst for the national movement.

Dr. King had rallied with the Memphis community on behalf of the striking workers less than a week before, but returned again on April 3. Because he was feeling ill, King initially stayed behind at the motel and sent word that he was not well enough to attend and speak at the rally. The disappointment of the crowd was so palpable, however, that the rally leaders called and convinced Dr. King to come and say a few words. The world is a better place as a result of Dr. King being convinced to speak that night, because it is clear to me that his extemporaneous words were steeped in an eternal perspective and specifically suited to penetrate the deep need of the culture.

With the benefit of hindsight, Dr. King's words also seem to carry a bit of premonition about his mortality. He spoke about the promised land and how he might not get there with those gathered. He admitted to having the usual desire to live a long life, but he also embraced the notion that it was likely not going to be the reality for him. It seemed as though Dr. King realized the work to which he was called would cost him his life in the end.

He was correct. Dr. King was assassinated the very next day on the balcony of his motel. His off-the-cuff words from the night before are the very last recorded words we have from him.

They are words that reverberate to this day, especially the closing paragraph:

> Well, I don't know what will happen now. We've got some dif-
> ficult days ahead. But it doesn't matter with me now. Because
> I've been to the mountaintop. And I don't mind. Like anybody,
> I would like to live a long life. Longevity has its place. But
> I'm not concerned about that now. I just want to do God's
> will. And He's allowed me to go up to the mountain. And
> I've looked over. And I've seen the promised land. I may not
> get there with you. But I want you to know tonight, that we,
> as a people, will get to the promised land. And I'm happy,
> tonight. I'm not worried about anything. I'm not fearing any
> man. Mine eyes have seen the glory of the coming of the Lord.[1]

"I've been to the mountaintop." Those five words speak compellingly to our universal longing for achievement and exhilaration. They indicate a high that comes from having "arrived." It is what we mean when we say we have had a "mountaintop experience." But while Dr. King's usage of the phrase does invoke some of these meanings, they clearly invoke another as well—one that is described in the words that follow. It is a description that reveals Dr. King's eternal perspective—a perspective best embodied by his utterance, "I've looked over."

It is clear to me that one of Dr. King's greatest gifts was an ability to set his eyes on the eternal while the world around him was simmering, boiling, and embroiled in chaos. He was able to mentally focus on the things that would have a lasting impact. And he was able to do it because God had taken him to the proverbial mountaintop and allowed him to look over into what would be. Like the story of Moses, to which Dr. King was no doubt eluding, God had afforded him a view of the promised land from atop the mountain, and that is what gave him hope and inspiration in what would have otherwise been a very dark place. It is also what made his time on earth so impactful.

Friends, the main impact of our lives is always going to occur where our eyes are set. If our eyes are set on material gain or personal fame, our greatest impact will very likely be in those areas. That would be hollow enough were it only for how fleeting those gains and fame are in this hot-now-but-forgotten-tomorrow world, but it turns downright tragic when we consider that this kind of impact is confined to this temporal world. It just simply will not last.

Brooke and I have a slightly sardonic way of reminding ourselves about this reality. In a moment of decision, one of us will say, "We are going to be dead soon," or "We won't be around to find out if this works." I admit it sounds a bit dark, and we say it more than a little tongue-in-cheek, but the reminder serves a specific purpose. We both understand the intent behind the words, and we both desire to make decisions that will last in the long run. We are trying to remind ourselves that our earthly bodies and possessions do not meet that definition—they simply will not last. It is a way to nudge each other toward decisions that will carry more weight in eternity.

The allure of the temporal is strong for all of us. I spend far too much time mentally consumed by my checkbook, my physical body, my shelter, my clothing, and my image. I think it is fair to say we all do.

But what if we could learn to constantly look over? What if we could build a habit of regularly setting our eyes on His fame rather than our own? What if we could fully grasp our ability to make an impact on the eternal from our current places in the temporal? What if our energy and devotion were channeled into things that will last beyond our lifetimes, or even beyond this earth's existence?

Ironically, achieving that shift and setting our eyes on the eternal will dramatically improve our ability to amplify the fame of our God in the here and now. Taking our eyes off of the temporal and going up to the mountaintop to look over does more to unleash our impact on this side of heaven than anything we can do of our own volition and strength.

Paul's admonition to the church at Colossae was to "set your hearts on things above . . . Set your minds on things above, not on earthly things," but we know from Paul's life and the rest of his writing that he believed fervently in the duty of the church to make an impact on the larger society. Far from calling believers out of engagement with the world around them, Paul was reminding the church that the best way to make an impact on this world is to set our eyes on the next. If our eyes are on the world around us, the weight of our fallen nature will encumber us. But if we are able to look over, and to set our eyes on the eternal, the weight of our God's fame will begin to overwhelm that fallen nature that surrounds us.

TO DIE IS GAIN

I will be glad to slip the bonds of earth. I do not mean that to sound morbid, and there is so much for which I am thrilled to be living. But when my time comes and the work I am responsible for is complete, I will also be relieved to leave behind the very real bonds and burdens of this temporary home. This is a fragile mental balance that I want to steward carefully, because God has given us a sacred and wonderful duty to care for this temporary home, and we should by no means dismiss or diminish the importance of that charge (Gen. 1:28). In fact, one of the most significant reasons we are to look over into the eternal and set our eyes on things that will last is to magnify our effectiveness on this side of heaven.

In the lives of Abraham, Noah, Moses, Habakkuk, and Dr. King, we see specific examples of God's revealing a bit of the eternal and doing so for a purpose that is to be accomplished in the temporal. In each case, a major reason for revealing what would come was to motivate and inspire the work God was about to assign. It is as though the Creator knew that the task He was about to assign would come with a weight that would be too much to bear if it were not lightened by a knowledge of what would follow. So the Creator gave His created a glimpse of the "why." He gave them a peek into His master plan for their existence and called them not to lay down their burden but to carry it willingly for the purpose of His plan.

To Abraham, He showed a mighty nation (Gen. 12:1–4).

To Noah, He showed a fresh start for the world (Gen. 6:11–14).

To Moses, He used a literal mountaintop to show off the promised land (Num. 27:12–14; Deut. 34:1–4).

To Habakkuk, he bestowed strength to persevere through tremendous adversity (Hab. 3:19).

To Dr. King, He used a figurative mountaintop to show off the promised land.

In the case of Moses and Dr. King, it is worth noting that

their glimpse into the promised land was as much a reward for their faithfulness as it was motivation to be faithful. Each of them was taken into the eternal shortly after having been afforded a glimpse of it. Neither of them experienced the reward of the promised land in this life.

In the case of Abraham, the full realization of a mighty nation would come well after his death.

And in the case of Noah and Habakkuk, each would have to walk through widespread calamity and destruction before realizing the promise of God.

No matter what our glimpse into the eternal may be, it is the act of choosing the things of the eternal that make us effective for His fame here on earth. It is what enables us to move from a place of being eager to shed the bonds of earth to one of desperation to use the precious little time we have been given here to its fullest. A deeper understanding of what is to come will lead to a more fervent desire to redeem our time in the present.

The apostle Paul embodied this idea magnificently. He was imprisoned on account of the gospel numerous times and regularly admitted to the affliction it caused him.[2] Even so, his words sound extremely similar to Dr. King's:

> For to me, to live is Christ and to die is gain. If I am to go on living in the body, this will mean fruitful labor for me. Yet what shall I choose? I do not know! I am torn between the two: I desire to depart and be with Christ, which is better by far; but it is more necessary for you that I remain in the body. Convinced of this, I know that I will remain, and I will continue with all of you for your progress and joy in the faith, so

that through my being with you again your boasting in Christ
Jesus will abound on account of me. (Phil. 1:21–26)

"To live is Christ and to die is gain . . . I desire to depart and
be with Christ . . . I know that I will remain." Paul was essentially
saying, "It would be better for me if I were to leave this life now,
but I am choosing to stay with you because it is better for you
and for the gospel. I am choosing to stay because I have looked
over into the eternal, and I know that being with you is what is
necessary to achieve what I have seen."

Is it better to die? One day, certainly. But our Creator placed
us here not by chance but to fulfill a very specific mission. Yes, we
must set our eyes on the eternal, but as long as He has placed us in
this temporary home, we are tasked with setting our hands toward
having an impact on it. We set our eyes on the eternal not because
we are abandoning our current home, but because we know He has
called us to reach those who are in it. Our vision of the eternal is
to be used for the benefit of those who have not yet seen it.

AS IT WAS FORETOLD

My friend Senator James Lankford has a beautiful way of describing how our work on earth fits into the eternal framework. His
description speaks specifically to me as it is rooted in terms that
match my profession, but it is equally applicable no matter your
profession. The senator links our duty to tell of God's fame not
only to the story of Jesus but even further back to the *foretelling*
of the Savior! His reminder is that the foretelling is linked to the
life of Jesus and by extension linked to our retelling of it.

This linkage is rooted in the litany of times the first four chapters of Matthew reference the prophetic words of the Old Testament prophets. Depending on your translation, these instances (and others in the Gospel accounts) are prefaced with words like, "As it was written," or "To fulfill the words of the prophet," or my personal favorite, "As it was foretold."

The entire life of Jesus is a fulfillment of the prophecies that were given before Him. In the first four chapters of Matthew alone, we find the following fulfillments of prophecy about Jesus:

- Virgin birth (Matt. 1:22–23; Isa. 7:14)
- Birthplace of the Messiah (Matt. 2:5–6; Mic. 5:2–4)
- Called out of Egypt (Matt. 2:15; Hos. 11:1)
- Slaughter of firstborn sons (Matt. 2:16–18; Jer. 31:15)
- Preceded by John the Baptist (Matt. 3:3; Isa. 40:3)
- Geographic region for Jesus's ministry (Matt. 4:13–16; Isa. 9:1)

In each instance, the story of Jesus is carrying out the word that has been sent down before Him. In a very literal sense, the fame of Jesus has come before Him and prepared a way. But really, the entire narrative is a fulfillment of Isaiah 9:6: "For to us a child is born, to us a son is given, and the government will be on his shoulders. And he will be called Wonderful Counselor, Mighty God, Everlasting Father, Prince of Peace."

It speaks so powerfully to the question, Why am I on this earth?

My friends, the very Son of God was sent to this place we call our home. He was sent as a child—a young mother's son—with a mission that carried the weight of the world. He was given a name that encompassed all the might of His heavenly Father. But the reason He was sent is the same reason He has now sent us: to reach a lost and dying world.

"The government will be on his shoulders." Does this mean that governments of men will be capable of meeting all of society's ills? Certainly not. But just as certain, it is cause to engage those governments.

"He will be called Wonderful Counselor." Do we have all the answers? Certainly not. But the One who is in us just as certainly does.

"He will be called . . . Mighty God." Do we have might on our own? Certainly not. But we are invited to possess a power and a fame that transcends all others.

"He will be called . . . Everlasting Father." Will this world last forever? Certainly not. But we have the secret that will enable those around us to live forever with the Father.

"He will be called . . . Prince of Peace." Can we, in our own power, provide the peace that passes all understanding? Certainly not. But He not only can; He has promised that He will (Phil. 4:7).

All of this has already been foretold. We have been afforded the chance to "look over." What we have been shown has become our mission while we remain on this side of eternity. We are here to carry the fame of the One the prophets foretold. The One who came to us as a child, died with our sins upon His back, left His Spirit with us, and will return again one day.

Until that glorious day, our charge is to proclaim His fame:

"Lord, I have heard of your fame."

PART II

. . . .

THE LEGEND

Parents tell their children
about your faithfulness.
—ISAIAH 38:19

CHAPTER 5

. . . .

THE AWE FACTOR

When I consider your heavens,
the work of your fingers,
the moon and the stars,
which you have set in place,
what is mankind that you are mindful of them,
human beings that you care for them?

—PSALM 8:3-4

Why am I not in awe?

It is a question I find myself regularly asking. How is it that I profess to believe in a God whose love reaches to the heavens, and His faithfulness to the skies (Ps. 36:5), and yet I often feel unloved?

How is it possible my God set the moon and stars in place, and yet I doubt His ability to intervene in my daily circumstances (Ps. 8:3)?

Why is it that a God whose name and praise reaches to the ends of the earth (Ps. 48:10) so often feels missing from my little corner of the planet?

If it is true that He cares for me so deeply He has numbered the hairs of my head (Luke 12:7), why do I so often think I have escaped His notice?

The questions are endless, and it is likely you ask them as well. But they all really boil down to the simple question of whether or not what we profess to believe about our God has permeated beyond our heads and our mouths and into a practical application that flows from our hearts into our everyday lives. It is a question about whether or not we have truly encountered His fame. It is a fame that is exceedingly large, excruciatingly small, completely inexhaustible, and yet fully attainable. In fact, it is promised to us.

So why am I not in awe? Is it because I doubt who He is? Or do I doubt what He has promised? Or maybe it is that I question the validity of my call to participate in His magnificent work? Maybe I have difficulty believing that a God of this fame would choose to fulfill His promises through me. Perhaps that is why I do not stand in awe.

Regardless of the reason, it is time for that to change. It is time for you and me to glimpse the sheer magnitude of our God and still run toward His vastness.

It is time for us to comprehend the incomprehensible idea that the same vast God who set the moon and stars in place has stooped down to embrace the smallness of our lone beings and has called us into His magnificent plan.

It is time for us to deal with the reality that what we know about God is infinitesimally small and will remain so for as long as we are bound to this earth.

It is time for us to claim the promise that our imaginations and comprehension cannot contain what He is about to do, and that He is about to do it through us.

Our God is beyond big.

But He is also less than small.

His complexity is incomprehensibly unknowable.

And yet His fame—in all its grandness, smallness, and mystery—has been promised to us small beings in ways we are not even capable of believing. In fact, maybe that is the answer. Maybe I am not in awe because I am so woefully incapable of unraveling the complexity and magnitude of my God. Or maybe I have yet to fully embrace His fame? Maybe I am frightened by the prospect of coming face-to-face with it. Whatever the cause, I am ready to chart a new path. I desire to encounter more of His fame. I desperately want to lay claim to the promise that all of it is available to me, for me, and through me.

BEYOND BIG

Our God is beyond big. In many ways, this is a concept that feels almost futile to write about, because at its very core is the reality that God's greatness is unknowable. It is unattainable—at least intellectually. The magnitude of His size and power is such that even the pinnacle of His creation—you and me—cannot know it. We want to define it in terms we understand: huge, awesome, all-powerful. But the truth is that those terms barely begin to describe the limits of our own understanding and do not even scratch the surface of God's magnitude.

Francis Chan gave an illustration of this idea in a brief video widely available on the Internet.[1] In it he shows a series of views of earth from increasingly distant perspectives: treetops, mountaintops, and eventually pulling farther and farther into space. Eventually, we lose sight of earth. Then we lose sight of the Milky Way galaxy. Eventually, the view of the cosmos is such that even our massive galaxy is invisible against the magnitude of creation. It seems impossible that the Creator of it all would care about life forms on one tiny planet inside of one now-invisible galaxy. The illustration gives just a glimpse of a God who is beyond big.

It also fires my imagination about what it must have sounded like when the thunderous voice of God boomed through the void, creating space and time to form a tangible and visible world with massive galaxies and microscopic atoms.

I must admit it is beyond my understanding to grasp the "how" of that moment. I do not comprehend how an interaction—no matter how powerful—with a void can produce something tangible. I do find it more than a little ironic, however, that one of the most prominent secular theories for the beginning of time rests on a premise of an explosive cacophony of sound in the ether. It seems to me this theory—as wild as it sounds—is actually a simplistic description of what Genesis 1 tells us.

The earth was formless and empty.

Darkness was over the surface of the deep.

The Spirit of God was hovering.

And then God . . . spoke.

I cannot tell you exactly how that tremendous sound interacted with the space-time continuum, or how the resulting collisions of those sound waves formed atoms and protons and neutrons—much less planets and galaxies! But I think it is safe to say it was an explosion of sound beyond any that had previously occurred, and beyond any that have occurred since.

It is the first demonstration we have of the stunning fame of our God. It is His fame embodied in the voice of the Creator. It is a booming sound with the power to destroy indiscriminately, and yet it is utilized in a fashion that established both the foundation of the heavens and the atoms of my being.

It leads to only one conclusion: My God is beyond big. His fame is immense, and I should stand in awe.

LESS THAN SMALL

My God is less than small.

We are conditioned to understand that the bigger and more powerful someone or something is, the less that person or entity can relate to regular people. We are conditioned to believe this because we see examples of it all around us.

The billionaire does not know how to shop for groceries or the price of a gallon of milk.

The politician is disconnected from the struggles of the factory worker or the parent working two jobs.

The giant company is forced to relinquish most of its personal interaction with its customers simply because of its increased size.

Even the friend who made it big is now too busy to interact with us.

We simply live in a world where bigger and more important nearly always means less direct interaction with the (seemingly) insignificant. Bigger means set apart. It means being separated from those who have not made it. In plenty of cases, some of this is unavoidable. But it is also so very often a choice. Our human nature is such that if we are offered an escape from interaction with the unlovely or the insignificant, we are eager to take it. If we have the chance to remove ourselves from situations where people are struggling, we jump at the opportunity.

There are exceptions, of course, and I will highlight a few of them. But as a general rule, as a person's influence and significance increase, their attention to and concern for the less significant decreases.

But not the God of the universe.

Not the God whose love reaches to the heavens.

Not the God whose faithfulness stretches to the skies.

Not the God who set the moon and stars in place.

Not the God whose name and praise extend to the ends of the earth.

Not the God whose voice rumbled through the void in such a way that His fame was revealed in the creation of all that is tangible.

No, that God did not grow distant as His power and glory increased and was made known. It was just the opposite. That God—the One adorned in all power and splendor—left His place on high to stoop down and give Himself for us. That God—the One who owns the cattle on a thousand hills—insisted on pursuing insignificant me. He insisted on pursuing insignificant you. That God—the One so big the galaxies He holds in place outnumber the sands of the shores—also cares for me to the point of numbering the hairs on my head.

It is really the greatest miracle of all. The God whose

magnitude cannot even begin to be measured or fathomed has chosen to make you and me the center of His ambition.

My God is beyond big. But He is also less than small.

INCOMPREHENSIBLY UNKNOWN

Our God is beyond big. He is less than small. And yet somehow, He is also still incomprehensibly beyond the reach of our wildest imaginations. The vast majority of His creation and His character still lie well outside the boundaries of our intellect and understanding. What we know about God feels infinitely large. But what we do not know about God and His fame is truly infinite. It is by definition incomprehensible. In fact, I really believe our answer to so many questions about God should be, "I know in part" (1 Cor. 13:12).

One of my favorite illustrations of God stooping down to make a tiny portion of His greatness available to us is a conversation the great inventor George Washington Carver had with God. Carver retold the conversation this way:

One day I went into my laboratory and said, "Dear Mr. Creator, please tell me what the universe was made for." The Great Creator answered, "You want to know too much for that little mind of yours. Ask something more your size, little man." Then I asked, "Please, Mr. Creator, tell me what man was made for." Again the Great Creator replied, "You are still asking too much." So then I asked, "Please, Mr. Creator, will you tell me why the peanut was made?" "That's better," God answered, "what do you want to know about the peanut?"[2]

As you may know, Carver would go on to discover a seemingly endless number of uses for the tiny peanut. These included using the peanut to make foods like soup, candy, and coffee. He found ways to use it as a cooking aid—including one method that made fried sweet potatoes taste like fried chicken! But he also used the peanut to make dyes, grease, medicine, soap, plant food, and even paper—just to name a few. All told, Carver discovered approximately three hundred uses for the peanut. He would attribute these revolutionary discoveries to the fact that his mighty God—and the creator of the peanut—drew near to him in order to reveal just a fraction of His wondrous ways. The God of infinite fame opened Carver's mind to understand the many beautiful attributes of the tiny peanut He had created.

But if God had all of that in mind for the peanut, what do you imagine He has in store for you, the pinnacle of His creation?

This is a God whose visible greatness is beyond our capacity to understand, and whose invisible greatness is incomprehensibly and unknowably greater still.

Even so, it is a God who makes our hearts His home, and who desires nothing more than to be pursued by the ones He created and the ones He called "very good" (Gen. 1:31). He has made Himself small in order to inhabit our beings and be the object of our affection.

It is truly a miracle. But I beg of you not to stop with being amazed and astounded by these two seemingly juxtaposed characteristics of God. Instead, ask of Him the "why" question. Why, O God, have You done this magnificent thing, and placed me at the center of it? Why have You shown us a glimmer of Your greatness, and yet also reduced Yourself to a place where I might know You? In the words of King David: "What is mankind that you are mindful of them, human beings that you care for them?" (Ps. 8:4).

For as long as we are on this side of heaven, we will know only in part. And yet I believe the promise that was made to Habakkuk is available for us as well, and that there is infinitely more of God's fame available to us. In fact, it is not merely available to us, but was intended for us and is promised to us.

My God is beyond big. He is less than small. He is incomprehensibly unknowable.

We know only in part.

There is so much more available and promised to us.

He is preparing to do more than we could ever imagine.

THE FAME PROMISE

Our family lives in an old split-level home. Because of its age, there are the typical signs of settling: slightly uneven floors, walls that are less than perfectly square, and the occasional mortar cracks in the exterior brick. But all in all, the foundation of our home has stood the test of time. It remains solid and, until recently, showed no real signs of losing its impenetrability to the elements.

But this past year brought with it more rain than I have ever known. By at least one measure, the DC area had more heavy rain last year than any year in recorded history. It not only rained consistently, but it rained in volumes that seem impossible. On one particular day, it rained three inches in an hour at our property. And that was after a week of nearly constant rain. On top of all the rain, our neighborhood is situated such that much of the surrounding area drains through it as water seeks to find its way to the Potomac River. It means that our neighborhood is one of the last to dry out after a storm—or in this case, storm after storm after storm.

The historic amounts of rain and the previously unknown levels of ground saturation tested the integrity of every home in the neighborhood. Nearly every property had some example of this—a flooded basement, a leaky roof, or a plugged drain. We were fortunate. We had only very light water seepage at one corner of our lower level, as well as a bit of water that found its way into the garage and kitchen due to door seals I needed to repair.

But the seepage into the lower level got me thinking. Why was it that a home proven to be impenetrable for the last several decades was now showing signs of being penetrable? Why was it that walls that had previously repelled the water were now suddenly being breached? Why were the seams of those walls no longer able to hold?

The answer, of course, is that the walls of our home had never before been asked to withstand that much water. They had never been tested to that extent. It was an occurrence for which they had not been measured.

I firmly believe that you and I are on the edge of that same moment. We are on the edge of the moment when the God who is beyond big and less than small is about to reveal even more of His incomprehensibly unknown. He is about to embark on the fame promise He made to Habakkuk: "Look at the nations and watch—and be utterly amazed. For I am going to do something in your days that you would not believe, even if you were told" (Hab. 1:5).

The fame of our God is about to pour down in volumes we cannot measure. It is going to confound us because it will not comport with the limits of God we have previously known. It will contain a new sliver of that incomprehensible and inexhaustible fame.

But most important, it is going to pour down in such measure that the walls we have built will no longer be able to keep it out. It is about to rush in through the seams of our life. It is, in fact, designed for the very purpose of permeating our defenses. It cannot be contained, and I do not wish to contain it. He is preparing to make more of His fame known, and He is looking for those who are eager to dedicate their lives to the revelation of that fame.

Our God is beyond big.

He is less than small.

We know but a tiny part of His complexity. He is incomprehensibly unknowable.

But a greater dose of His fame is coming. And our walls will not be able to contain it!

CHAPTER 6

· · · ·

I DON'T KNOW

*"What no eye has seen, what no ear
has heard, and what no human mind
has conceived"—the things God has
prepared for those who love him.*
—1 CORINTHIANS 2:9

We have an irrational fear of the unknown. Actually, it may not be irrational for those who do not profess to believe in the God of the incomprehensibly unknown. If that is you, it makes perfect sense to have some trepidation about setting your foot in an unfamiliar place and one in which you have no assurance the ground will be steady.

But for those of us who claim to believe in a God who

supersedes and surpasses the bounds of our human minds, it is at the very least inconsistent to walk in fear of the unknown. It is a fear we need to unlearn. We need to unlearn it primarily because the unknown is where the mystery of God abides. The unknown is where we just might discover a bit more of His fame and glory. Venturing into the unknown will enable us to encounter more of God. Surely that is what we should desire!

So how do we shake the tendency to view the mystery of the unknown with trepidation? How do we instead embrace with exhilaration the understanding that God's greatness is more fully discovered when we challenge the boundaries of our own understanding?

I think the first step lies in a renewal of our willingness to say, "I don't know." Too often, we—and most certainly I—have desperately searched for ways to never have to admit we are lacking an answer. Whether it is in our relationships, our education, or our professions, admitting we do not know has become taboo because it is perceived to be a sign of personal weakness. So we avoid admitting we do not know at all costs.

But if our goal is to unleash and participate in the fame of our God, we must turn this mind-set on its head. On the most basic level, we must realize anew that our very salvation rests on an acknowledgement that we are lacking and in need of a Savior. We undercut that profession when we stubbornly refuse to admit there are times we do not have the answer. But even beyond that, if we are in pursuit of a revelation of God's fame in our lives, does that not necessitate a searching out of the greatness of God that we do not yet know? Does it not require our willingness to go beyond what we know? How can we possibly do that if we continue to insist we have all the answers?

Sure, the idea of believing in a God so huge we cannot fathom His greatness is intoxicating. But if we truly want to move beyond ideas that intoxicate us and into lives actually infused with His power, we must acknowledge it will take something beyond our own power and intellect. We must get comfortable saying, "I don't know."

I want to learn how to not only be unafraid of admitting I don't know but in fact learn to be excited to say it! If we can move to a mental state of longing to live in that kind of dependence, we will begin to tap into the power of God. We will begin to uncover the mystery of God's fame that lies in the unknown. We will see how much more He can do with our inability than we can do in our own ability.

Let us be desperate for that. Let us be excited and eager to say, "I don't know," and to venture into those areas where it is obvious that only God can come through for us.

HOW BIG IS HIS STORY?

Speaking of venturing into deep waters, I am going to ask a question that will shock many of your theological sensibilities and tempt you to stop reading. It will do so because it will challenge what you have likely always believed and suggest a certain amount of impossibility for fully ascertaining a complete answer. But regardless of the extent to which you agree or disagree with the appropriateness of this next question, I encourage you to stick with me as we explore it. I think it just might cause all of us to acknowledge how much we do not know and motivate us to press deeper into the mystery of our God. Are you ready? Here goes!

How many planets and galaxies does the love of salvation reach?

Are you still reading? I know that many of you will be tempted to quit exploring here and for a very understandable reason: the Bible gives us a very precise account of creation. It is an account rooted in six days of creating and one day of rest. It has a clear beginning and a clear ending, and it only specifically references one inhabited planet—ours. It is an account I believe in without exception. I believe the heavens and the earth—and all that live in them—were created when the all-powerful God spoke during the course of those six days. I accept it as truth—even the parts I cannot square with reality in my finite human brain.

But I also believe fervently in 1 Corinthians 13:9–12, which states in no uncertain terms that there are mysteries of our God that vastly surpass our ability to comprehend them. They vastly exceed our ability to see them. And in fact, they vastly exceed the bounds of what God has chosen to reveal to us. Depending on the version, it says we "see dimly" or as "a reflection in a mirror." The passage closes with this rather unequivocal expression of our intellectual inadequacy: "Now I know in part; then I shall know fully, even as I am fully known."

So, in what would be just one of an infinite number of examples, is it possible that God has revealed to us but a fraction of His creation and salvation story? Is it possible that the "heavens" include additional iterations of God's love story with His creation? Is it possible that we, the pinnacle of His creation, do not even begin to understand the limits of His creation?

I hope you can predict my answer.

"I don't know."

I simply do not know. I do not know whether the Genesis story tells us everything about the elements of creation for which God would make a salvation plan. I am not even trying to advance one theory or another. I simply do not know whether 1 Corinthians 13:9–12 suggests there is more to that particular story. But I use the example to make this point: I *do* know it is possible. I do know that we can have certainty about the idea that there is more to God's story than He has currently revealed to us. I do know that He has chosen to keep much of His wonder and His fame veiled. I do know that He has done so in order that we might persistently seek Him out. I do know that there is more of Him for all of us to discover if we will simply choose that pursuit over settling for our preconceived assumptions.

After all, knowing the answer to this question is not really the point. The point—and the pursuit—is to know more of God. It is to know more of His fame. Let us desire the goal—knowing Him more—above our desire to cling to our long-held assumptions.

One day we will know fully. It is a promise for this question about the scope of creation and for countless other questions. Until then, we have every reason to eagerly search out the unknown. Our fear of the unknown is misguided and needs to be unlearned. It needs to be unlearned because the unknown is where the mystery and the fame of our all-powerful God abide. The unknown is where a greater revelation of His identity waits to be discovered. Does that greater revelation include a reach of salvation that extends beyond what He has revealed to us?

Guess what? I don't know.

CONFRONTING GOD

It is one thing to begin to get a sense of the vastness of God's fame. It is another still to begin to accept that His fame extends wildly into the unknown. But how do we begin to tap into that vast fame? How do we find a way to explore the vast unknown that contains more of God's fame, power, and mystery? If we want a new revelation of God's fame and we are convinced it lies in an experience with God that is beyond what we know, then how do we encounter it? How do we find it? How do we call it out?

Habakkuk discovered the answer. Habakkuk received his mission and his marching orders. How? By confronting his God. By taking his frustration, his doubt, and his problems directly to the almighty God and insisting on God's intervention.

Too often I have been unwilling to engage in this kind of confrontation. I have believed that confronting the all-knowing God will suggest a challenge to His authority. The truth is just the opposite: He longs for an invitation to share a greater portion of His plan. More specifically, He longs for us to inquire of Him—and even question Him about our doubts—because He desires to reveal Himself to us by doing a work through us. After all, that is precisely why He created us.

He does not wish to hide His fame. No, He is desperate to reveal it. But He has already chosen the way in which that will be accomplished, and it is through the lives of His people. It begins when His people recall the power and fame of their God. It continues when His people get desperate enough for more of their God that we confront Him and insist on more of Him. And it is realized when the fame of the almighty God becomes the ultimate mission of His people. It begins when you and I get so desperate to live for the single aim of His glory that we are willing to overcome our fear and confront our God with the challenges standing in our way.

If we want to see God's fame, we must step forward into the line of duty.

If we want to see God's fame, we must be willing to embrace the tension of confronting Him.

If we want to see God's fame, we must find the courage to insist that He reveal Himself.

We must shed the feeling and the fear that confronting Him is presumptuous. Far from presumptuous, it is what He desires! We were created for the purpose of glorifying Him. He wants nothing more than to embrace all of us—our belief, our doubt, and our challenges—in order to have real relationship with us, and to make more of Himself known to us and to the world around us.

Confronting our God is not insisting we know better. It is admitting we cannot see the fullness of His plan and are frustrated by the things we see that seem to be void of His presence. It is asking Him for a greater revelation of His plan for those areas of our frustration. It is going to Him with an expectation that He has a plan and that He will reveal it to us. And it is preparing ourselves for the likelihood that His plan for providing an answer for those areas of frustration includes us.

His plan is, in fact, us.

Confronting God means admitting we are not okay with what we see around us and being willing to take those misgivings to God. But it also means being willing to step up and be used when God's response is a solution that He intends to achieve through us.

Are you ready to confront your God?

Are you ready to step into the line of duty?

Are you ready for Him to lead you into the unknown in order to experience more of Him?

Are you ready to take more of His fame into the world in order for brokenness to be made whole again?

That is what it will take. He is big enough to handle our confrontation. He is eager to accept our doubt. But in order to reveal more of Himself to us, He demands our participation.

You see, His mystery and His fame are shrouded for a reason. They are shrouded because they are reserved for those who would seek them out. They are reserved for those who would give their lives to find them. They are withheld and set apart for those who would step forward and actively participate in making them known.

Are you ready to lift that veil? Can you be trusted with more of God's fame? Are you committed to using the influence of your life to amplify what will be entrusted to you? If so, I challenge you to confront the almighty God. He has promised to meet you in that place.

WHY MY STORY?

Maybe you can see the big view—the wide view—of God's fame. Maybe you have reached a place of acceptance about the depth and the breadth of the almighty God. Maybe you embrace the idea that He is vast and we are not.

If so, that is a good place to be. It is a good place, but it is not the destination. For you see, to be an active participant in the move of God's fame, we must do more than grasp the big view. We must also identify and embrace the small view. We must personalize the truth that our story—no matter how small it feels—plays an integral role in that big story. We must visualize that His vastness is manifest through an army of His people committed to reflecting His fame through their lives.

That is how a small life becomes a part of His vast fame, by intertwining it with others committed to the same task: making Him known.

Habakkuk felt small. His problems felt vast. Despite it all, he found the courage to confront his God and insist on His mighty intervention. But what was it that finally triggered a response from his God? What was it that finally caused the silence and the separation from God's engagement to come to an end?

It was the fact that Habakkuk finally moved to insert his small story into the vast story of the Almighty's. It was the result of a proactive decision by Habakkuk to be a part of the solution rather than simply a mouthpiece for the problem. Listen to Habakkuk's forceful statement: "I will stand at my watch and station myself on the ramparts; I will look to see what he will say to me, and what answer I am to give to this complaint" (Hab. 2:1).

Not only did Habakkuk decide to engage and become part of the story, but he also insisted on an answer. There is a stubborn tone to Habakkuk's words and a resolute nature to his actions. He has decided where he fits in. He has chosen the place on which he will make his stand, and he is resolute in his commitment to stand firm until he has heard from God.

Habakkuk is in. He is standing watch. He is guarding the ramparts. Come what may, Habakkuk is in the fight.

That action is what triggered God's response, which followed quickly after Habakkuk's action: "Then the LORD replied: 'Write down the revelation and make it plain on tablets so that a herald may run with it'" (Hab. 2:2).

God had a plan. He had a message for the world—and a message for the perpetrators of injustice. But he wanted to communicate that message through Habakkuk. He had infused Habakkuk with an ability to clearly communicate for this very purpose. He wanted Habakkuk to translate the revelation of His fame into words the people could plainly understand.

He intended for Habakkuk to be the way in which His incomprehensible and unknown fame would translate into a tangible world. And He chose Habakkuk specifically because his gifting—his story—was suited to the task.

Your story is suited to a specific task, as well. Your heritage—be it beautiful or broken—is not an accident. To the contrary, it has been orchestrated to prepare you for this time and this place. The question is simply, "Will you step to your watch and guard the ramparts?"

If you will, God will answer. He will speak to you from within your heritage and will put you on mission for His fame. He will incorporate your story into His story. He will use your story to lift His fame.

But the next move is yours.

Before He answers, you must step to your place on the wall.

In order to participate in the move of His mighty fame, you must first be at your watch.

CHAPTER 7

. . . .

HERITAGE

The living, the living—they praise you,
as I am doing today;
parents tell their children
about your faithfulness.
—ISAIAH 38:19

The shots that killed Joyce rang out on February 26, 1962. In an act of senseless violence, Joyce's husband took her life and then turned the weapon on himself. Joyce was just twenty-nine years old.

It would have been an unthinkable tragedy if the impact of this senseless violence had been contained there. It is horrific whenever innocent lives are taken, and it is compounded when a family member is the one responsible for the taking. The loss of Joyce at such a young age would no doubt be difficult for many in her world to process. But as is always true in these cases, the real impact of the senseless violence carried out that day would be borne by those left behind. The real struggle, and the real navigation of loss, would fall—as it often does—to the ones least deserving of and least prepared for it. It would fall to little Stevie and little Curtis.

Stevie was just eight years old when his mother was murdered, and Curtis was just five. Two young brothers who had already endured a biological father who was absent and unreliable, and a stepfather who had come and gone. Now, suddenly, a second stepfather had violently taken their mother from them. In the blink of an eye, Stevie and Curtis lost their mother, their home, and just about everything they knew. Everything that had been their reality in one moment was gone in the next. It is a circumstance that would bring the most stoic and mature among us to our knees. But it was not the stoic or the mature who were required to bear the brunt of this violence. It was eight-year-old Stevie and five-year-old Curtis.

In the days that followed, it was decided that Stevie and Curtis would live with their grandparents. There were aunts and uncles who offered to take the brothers in, but they were already raising families of their own, so Joyce's parents insisted they would be the ones to raise the boys. Carl was seventy-four years old, and Ida was sixty-six. Their child-rearing days were far behind them, and yet suddenly the primary purpose of their remaining years was the upbringing of two young boys who had just lost the core of their universe. Carl and Ida were, of course, also grieving the loss of their daughter, but life—as it is prone to do—marched on and presented them with a new and challenging hand to play.

Before I tell you more about the heroic life of Carl and Ida, I need to tell you how they fit into my heritage picture. You see, little Stevie is now Steve. His full name is Stevan Michael Bennett, and he is my dad. He is not only my dad, but he is also the father of my six siblings and the grandfather of nine (for now) grandchildren. He has a legacy that is everything his biological father's is not—one marked with devotion, presence, and consistency. It is a legacy that is growing by the year, and one that is passing along a godly heritage that will outlive him by countless generations.

Joyce is my grandma. She is the grandma I never knew, because she was taken from my dad and his brother when they were just boys. She was taken from all of us.

Carl Edgar Bennett is my heroic great-grandfather. Ida Belle (Curtis) Bennett is my heroine great-grandmother. Born in 1887 and 1895 respectively, Carl and Ida had already lived full lives that were typical to the rural farming areas of central Illinois. They had worked long and hard throughout the years to raise a family and maintain a simple lifestyle. They lived in a modest home in a small farming community, but I imagine they were able to reflect with satisfaction on a life that was mostly in the rearview mirror. It was at this stage that their lives were thrown several decades in reverse.

My dad will tell you that his grandpa and grandma gave little Curtis and him the first stable home they had ever known. After years of instability and then an unspeakable tragedy that would shake even the most stable among us, there was no more valuable gift Grandpa and Grandma Bennett could have given the two young boys. For more than a decade, Grandpa and Grandma provided that stability to Steve (at some point, the nickname

Stevie fell away) and Curt (Grandma always called him Curtis, though he would eventually go by Curt). Both boys would leave for college at age eighteen and then marry (my dad to my mom, Melody) in their early twenties. By this time, Grandpa was in his early nineties and Grandma her mideighties.

Grandpa and Grandma Bennett devoted the final active decade of their life to raising my dad and uncle. Even at a young age, I remember recognizing what a tremendous gift they were and what an enormous sacrifice they had made. I do not think they would use the word *sacrifice* because they loved little Stevie and Curtis and were eager to give them the very best they had to offer. Shortly after my dad and uncle came to live with them, Grandpa and Grandma moved from the farm into town and built a slightly larger house than they otherwise would have, because their would-be-retirement was now devoted to raising another family. So while Grandpa and Grandma may not have called it a sacrifice, it was a big one nonetheless. While most people their age were winding down their activity level, Grandpa and Grandma were pouring out their lives for two young boys who desperately needed them.

Grandpa lived to the ripe young age of ninety-nine. He remains a giant of a man in my mind—permanently etched as my five-year-old brain remembers him: stoic, handsome, and full of inner strength. He died on May 27, 1987—my sixth birthday. It is one of those few memories from my early years that remains vivid to this day and will remain so forever. I remember hearing the news and feeling the greatest sense of loss I had ever known. I walked out to our sandbox in the backyard, where I loved to play with toy trucks and bulldozers. I sat in the sand and wept bitterly.

Grandma lived to be ninety-four years old and went to be with her Creator in 1990. She was the legal guardian of both Uncle Curt and my dad. They would tell you she was the center of their childhood universe. She filled the mother void as well as anyone possibly could have. She was a tremendously strong woman—she had to be. She was not one to take guff from anyone, including her grandsons. But that strength gave her the fortitude to raise two boys in the twilight of her life. The oldest of those boys then married my mother and together with her raised my siblings and me.

I wish I could have known Grandma Joyce. Far more than that, I wish my dad had not had her torn away from him at such a young and tender age. No child should lose his or her mother— especially in that fashion. Even so, I marvel at the provision of a mighty God. Even in the face of unthinkable and insurmountable loss, He was making a way. He was preparing a legacy for my dad and his brother. He was readying a heritage and a legacy for generations to come. He was charting a path for many, including my dad, my Uncle Curt, my siblings, and me.

I have no way of knowing what that fateful day was like for Grandma Joyce. But I have to think her mother's heart was with little Stevie and little Curtis and that it was focused on a concern for their future. But their future was held by One much higher and secured by One the perils of this earth could not reach. He would protect the heritage that was to flow to and through them. Out of the evil that took Grandma Joyce would flow provision and redemption.

I am forever in the debt of Carl Edgar Bennett and Ida Belle Bennett—Grandpa and Grandma Bennett. It is because of their sacrifice that our family name is now Bennett rather than

Levandoski—a change my dad and Uncle Curt appropriately made some time after going to live with Grandpa and Grandma. I long to carry well the legacy and the heritage that accompanies the name Grandpa and Grandma passed down to me, and I yearn for the day when I will again embrace them in eternity. I have often imagined that rarely has the welcome into eternity been more heartfelt and fitting than it was for them.

"Carl, well done, good and faithful servant!"

"Ida, well done, good and faithful servant!"

Hearing that phrase said to me is my primary goal in life.

THE WORLD ON THE END OF A STRING

"Son, you've got the world on the end of a string!"

My Grandpa Candler's voice is loud, deep, and clear. It is the voice of an old-school Methodist minister and a deep-bass hymn singer, and its tone sounds as if it is perpetually coming from behind a pulpit. It sounds that way because it so often has resonated from behind a pulpit. But on this day, it came from the back of the little prop boat we were using to fish Burntside Lake, part of the enormous compilation of lakes that make up the boundary waters between northern Minnesota and Canada. It is Grandpa's favorite place on earth, and I have countless memories of summer weeks spent there with Grandma and him.

Possibly the most vivid are the times we played "shiver me timbers." When the weather was cold, my brothers and I, and sometimes a cousin or two, would sit in the makeshift steam sauna until we were good and toasty, and then make a mad dash outside into the frigid weather, down the dock, and leap into the icy lake—before scrambling out and sprinting back to the warmth of the sauna.

Grandpa and Grandma thought we were crazy for playing "shiver me timbers." Looking back, I can see that wisdom comes with age.

But on this day, we were fishing. Truthfully, Grandpa was always fishing when he was at the lake. He would rise before dawn, fish until breakfast, return to eat quickly, fish until lunch, return again to eat quickly, fish until dinner, return a third time to eat quickly, and then fish until dark. If he was at the lake, he wanted to be in the boat and on the lake. It was his haven, and I loved to go with him. I had to choose my spots wisely, however, because many of these excursions were very long for a young boy, and once that boat left the dock, it was not coming back until mealtime or bedtime.

And yes, on this chilly late-summer day, I did indeed have the world on the end of a string. My fishing line was irretrievably hooked on the lake bottom. It happened to me a lot, and I knew it was a source of genuine frustration for Grandpa. My inexperience was cutting into his favorite thing. My carelessness meant he had to put down his precious line, maneuver the boat to the other side of my line, and work to extract my line himself. He was annoyed, because for the next few minutes he would be at the lake but not fishing. That was practically a sin!

But as annoyed as he was, I was also keenly aware that including me in his favorite thing was infinitely more important to him than actually doing his favorite thing. It was more important to him that I gain experience and that we share quality time—often without words—than it was for him to relax. As important as the fishing and the relaxation were to him, I always knew I was more valued.

I also always knew what was *most* important to both Grandpa and Grandma—Jesus.

My Grandpa Candler pastored for forty-two years. Until he retired when I was fifteen, pastoring was core to his identity. I have countless memories of visiting the parsonage in Grand Ridge, Illinois, and of getting to walk across the yard to his church office to help him fold bulletins for Sunday's service. I remember sitting in the old pews on Sunday morning and listening to his voice thunder through the sanctuary. And I remember all the grandkids standing on the stage to sing a hymn together. I was, however, relegated to learning how to play the tune on the xylophone because my singing voice was so obnoxious. No joke—I was such a lousy singer I was not allowed to sing among the grandkids in my own grandfather's church! And a child playing the xylophone was somehow less annoying than that same child singing. Talk about a brutally honest life lesson.

Through all the memories, what I remember most is that Grandpa and Grandma's faith was always at the center. It was quite simply—and quite visibly—the platform upon which they built everything else. My grandpa's life was lived in service to the congregations he pastored, and there are untold numbers who will share eternity with their Savior because of him.

My grandma's service was possibly even nobler. As any pastor's spouse can tell you, her duties were innumerable. Everything from organizing social gatherings to caring for the needy and hosting congregants in her home fell into Grandma's portfolio. She did it all with love and grace and for each of those forty-two years.

In fact, even when we were at Burntside Lake, Grandma was serving. Grandpa (and whoever was with him) would return

from fishing, and Grandma would have all manner of delicious-
ness prepared. If it was mealtime, it was often fried fish—freshly
caught and cleaned by Grandpa the day before. If it was breakfast or snack time, it was often my personal favorite: homemade
cinnamon rolls right out of the oven. But either way, even on
vacation, Grandma was always serving. It was always about finding ways to bless those around her.

Between the two of them, the legacy of service and faithful
devotion they embodied created for me a heritage that is rich
beyond measure. Even today, they continue to give of what they
have and what they love. Just a few weeks ago, Grandpa gifted
me with some tools from his woodworking shop. I am most
excited about the planer, the biscuit joiner, and the collection of
pipe clamps. But, of course, there were also several boxes of his
woodworking magazines, dating back decades and meticulously
ordered and catalogued for easy reference.

After all, Grandpa never did like losing time. Even if it was
because I had the world on the end of a string.

BUILD ABOVE GROUND

Too many times, we lay a new foundation. Too many times, we
look back on what has been passed down to us and conclude it
must be discarded in favor of a fresh start. We decide there are
just too many blemishes in the foundation and that we can do
better on our own. So we reject our heritage and we go it alone.
We distance ourselves from those imperfect sinners who came
before us and set out to show the world how much better we
can do it.

To be fair, maybe the motive for casting aside the last generation's foundation is not always so nefarious. Maybe there is a good reason for pursuing a fresh start. But more than likely, your path to lifting high the fame of the Almighty runs through the experiences of those who have gone before you. Your opportunities to relate to the world around you are found in all the experiences—both good and bad—you have come through.

Each of us has inherited a foundation upon which we should be building God's fame. For some, the value is in a firm and solid foundation. I am so grateful that is the case as it pertains to my parents, Grandpa and Grandma Candler, and Great-Grandpa and Great-Grandma Bennett. What incredibly solid footing on which to stand and from which to build and proclaim.

I am doubly blessed because Brooke's heritage is also one of great service, the depths of which are difficult to adequately describe. Her parents, Dad and Mom Gambrell, have given their lives in service to the church, the needy, and especially the broken. Both have devoted decades to the task of pouring themselves out in order to meet the needs of the addict, the naked, the abused, and the homeless. They have restored the broken and embraced those who have been cast aside. Brooke's character contains an ability to recognize need that mine can only aspire to, and it does so specifically because of the imprint that Dad and Mom Gambrell's heritage has made on her. Our family is building on that foundation as well.

But for others, the value is found by rummaging through the wreckage for the purpose of making beauty from ashes (Isa. 61:3). The value comes in finding a heritage others have cast aside but that God has set aside. He has set it aside and preserved it for a specific purpose. David said it this way: "The stone the builders rejected has become the cornerstone" (Ps. 118:22).

When Grandma Joyce's young life was snuffed out, it should have sent crippling ripple effects down through the generations because it took a sledgehammer to the foundation of my dad's life. But because of the faithfulness of Grandpa and Grandma Bennett and my dad's determination to seize and build upon the solid foundation they provided for him, I have inherited a rich and solid foundation ready to be built upon. It is a foundation that includes wreckage and destruction but also redemption.

All these pieces come together to create a story worth telling. It is a flawed story, full of flawed people and brokenness—a brokenness clearly visible in me. But it is worth telling because it is my story with the markings of His saving grace all over it. It is worth telling because God has been working within the brokenness of the story to do a mighty work. He has been building His fame on top of the foundations—both the solid and the crumbling—of our lives.

You have a story, as well. You may think it speaks of tragedy and brokenness, and it does. All our stories do. But it does not speak *only* of tragedy and brokenness. It also speaks of a God whose fame is revealed when He reaches through that wreckage to restore the broken people within the carnage. Often, it is the brokenness that makes our stories worth telling. It is His restoration of our brokenness that makes our heritage worth building upon. After all, we are not trying to proclaim our perfection. We are trying to proclaim the fame of our God. The fame that continues to achieve perfection through our brokenness. The fame that works through the shattered circumstance that a murder-suicide creates, and moves an eight-year-old boy and his five-year-old brother from a lonely place to a stable place.

Your story likely does proclaim brokenness. But it also

proclaims His great fame, and it should be built upon rather than cast aside.

My heritage is a foundation worth building upon. Your heritage—your story—should also be built upon the foundation that has been passed down to you. Do not start over. Do not dig and build yet another foundation on the plot of the existing one. Use the foundation that those who have gone before you have laid, and take advantage of the cornerstone that others have cast aside.

Build above ground.

Build the first floor.

That is how the glory and the fame of God will be lifted high.

CHAPTER 8

. . . .

I AM WRONG

I will stand at my watch and station
myself on the ramparts;
I will look to see what he will say to me, and
what answer I am to give to this complaint.
—HABAKKUK 2:1

I hate to be wrong. While it is probably fair to conclude that most of us prefer not be proven wrong, this preference exists at unhealthy levels in me. In fact, I hate to be wrong so fervently that it is still a running joke among my siblings. We will be debating a topic (because that seems to be required in the Bennett family) and reach an impasse when a sibling (usually a brother) will say something like, "Well, Thann must be correct, because just ask him—he's never been wrong before!" Another brother will chime in, "True, there was that one time he thought he was wrong, but in the end decided he was mistaken about that and was actually correct after all."

It is said in jest and love, but the undertones of truth are still there. For as long as I can remember, I have had something close to an obsession with getting the answer correct. If I am honest with myself, I think it really has more to do with not being wrong than it does with actually being correct. I have a strong natural tendency to avoid at all costs getting the answer wrong, and certainly to avoid being wrong publicly. I know it is a character flaw and have worked intentionally over the years to reduce its presence in my life. Nevertheless, it remains one that my parents, siblings, and my bride will all readily attest still exists to this day. I simply cringe when I am wrong. I cringe twice as hard when I have to admit it out loud.

An ugly by-product of this fallen condition is that it requires I take pleasure in others being proven wrong. I tell myself this is not true and that I take no joy in seeing another fall. Quite frankly, if it were as simple as a choice between another falling or not, I might often pass the test. I might often genuinely prefer that others succeed. In fact, I am fairly confident I would usually pass the test at that level.

But if you and I have a disagreement, my being proven correct is by definition going to require you being proven wrong. And given the choice framed in that manner, I can assure you that my instinct will be one that craves—and too often delights in—your being proven wrong.

It is something I must overcome. You might think my need to overcome it stems from our call to humility and unselfishness, and that would certainly be true. But the stakes are really so much higher. The truth is that my ability to follow Habakkuk's example of engaging a vast God in and through my small life hangs in the balance of conquering this internal giant. Your ability to channel the fame, glory, and power of the Creator of the universe hinges on the same.

Why? Because channeling the fame of our God requires we step to our place on the ramparts. It requires we stand shoulder to shoulder with fellow followers of Jesus and trust them to engage with us. It requires giving them permission to be wrong occasionally—or even often—as they pursue and engage on behalf of a big God. It requires an acknowledgment that in the end our knowledge will be made full and our current state will be proven imperfect.

If we engage a big God and His fame now, we will look back from a future place and say conclusively, "I was wrong."

THE RAMPARTS

If we truly want to call the fame and power of our God into our time, we have to identify practical ways to place ourselves in a position to channel that fame. Habakkuk's story is a powerful illustration of the fact that God's fame hovers and smolders on the horizon. It is waiting. The reason for its wait is not so much that He has chosen to remain distant, but rather because we have chosen to hold it off. We have chosen not to carry it.

We have our own mix of reasons for this hesitation. Sometimes we do not believe it is real. Sometimes we are afraid of being the first or only one to channel it. Sometimes we are afraid of it altogether. But whatever the reason, we hang back rather than engage the smoldering fire that seeks to ignite and rush through the land.

For as powerful and plentiful as the Almighty's fame is, He has chosen to make its transportation dependent on us. He has chosen that its method for being passed down the line be through the hearts and souls of men and women. He has chosen for the mobility of His fame to rise and fall according to His people's willingness to possess it.

The first practical step we must take to possess His fame in our lives is to step to our watch on the ramparts. This must occur even if doubts persist, as we will discover shortly. But first, why do we need to position ourselves on the ramparts?

Merriam-Webster defines *rampart* as "a protective barrier," or "a broad embankment raised as a fortification and usually surmounted by a parapet."[1] Further, *parapet* is defined as "a low wall or railing to protect the edge of a platform, roof, or bridge."[2] Simply put, Habakkuk's rampart is a fortified wall at the edge of the territory upon which he can walk, and from which he can safely observe the surrounding area.

There are two observations that make this instruction significant. First, God called Habakkuk to stand on the very place where the eventual conflict would occur. From that vantage point, Habakkuk could observe the land and readily identify the approaching dangers. Similarly, God is calling us to position ourselves in the places of society where the eventual battles will be waged, and from those vantage places He is affording us a view of the coming threats.

Second, and more significant in my opinion, He is calling us to a specific place on the rampart. Other believers are called to separate and distinct places along the same wall. In order to complete the fortification He is calling us to, we must stand shoulder to shoulder with our brothers and sisters. You know, those brothers and sisters we are just sure are wrong. The ones who are equally sure *we* are wrong. God is not calling us to lay aside our pursuit of a more complete and accurate picture and knowledge of Him. But He is calling us to engage that pursuit shoulder to shoulder with those with whom we often disagree.

He is calling us to choose a unity in salvation and in His fame over a focus on division and disagreement. He is calling us to it in order that we might together observe the surrounding danger, and that we might together prepare for the coming clash.

We know that in the final day we will stand shoulder to shoulder with people of every tongue and every tribe to proclaim the glory of God (Rev. 7:9). We know there will be unity of purpose and understanding as we enter eternal glory. And yet we stand so divided now. Lines of division—theological, denominational, political, racial, societal, economic, and so forth—are everywhere we look. We often focus first on those differences rather than on our common Creator and Savior.

Here is the reality. Each of us will have to set aside an insistence on being proven correct if we are going to stand shoulder to shoulder on that rampart. Should we continue to pursue ultimate truth in all areas? By all means, yes! But by its very definition, achieving truth in unity in the end will require each of us having been wrong on some firmly held belief.

If we want to facilitate rather than hinder a move of God's fame, we have to step to our places on the rampart.

If we step to our places on the rampart, we must choose unity over insisting we are correct and the one next to us on the wall is wrong.

If we are going to successfully defend the land, each of us would do well to admit now, "I am wrong."

Let us work to show grace and choose unity in salvation even before we have the benefit of hindsight.

CONQUERING DOUBT

As we begin to move toward this concept of stepping up to facilitate a mighty move of God, we are going to face trepidation. I am sure of it for two main reasons.

First, until it becomes more ingrained in us, preparing to act while still on the near side of being convinced is thoroughly unnatural. It is not instinctive—at least not at first. We must build a habit in this area, and until then it will take conscious decision-making to override our hesitation.

Second, the Enemy will try to stop us. There is nothing that poses more of a threat to the forces of evil than the prospect of another believer stepping into the line of service and calling forth the power against which evil cannot stand. So when we make a decision to take our place on that wall, we must prepare ourselves physically, mentally, and especially spiritually. It is a move that must be bathed in prayer, because while it will revolutionize your life for the better, it is one—like most things worth doing—that will not be accomplished without resistance.

So how do we conquer our doubt and make decisions that are not supported by our culture? How do we gather the courage to act even when we are met with resistance in both the spiritual and the natural? In my experience, we have to flip the script and simply take the first step. Let me explain.

Mark Batterson has been my pastor for nearly twenty years. His voice—as well as his wife, Lora's—is reflected in these pages and in our family's life. In the foreword to my book *In Search of the King*, Mark wrote about one of my most significant experiences with overcoming doubt. He told how it took me nearly fifteen years to move from a place of receiving God's instruction to a place of taking the first concrete step of obedience by putting pen to paper.[3]

Fifteen years! That is an awfully long time to metaphorically stand behind the front lines while holding my armor. It is a long time to walk in disobedience, but I did so predominately for two reasons: 1) I had tremendous doubt, and 2) I had no idea how to start. In the end, both of these reasons had to be overcome internally, by accepting and deciding to act upon the fact that the power that was in me was greater than the power of my doubt or inability.

The doubt had to be conquered by deciding to act no matter the consequences, and I was only able to do that by giving all the results to God. I literally (and verbally) gave him responsibility for wherever this path would lead, be it good or bad. I would give Him credit if it succeeded, and yes, I might even blame Him if it went poorly. I think we often underestimate how much of our burden of doubt God is ready and willing to shoulder. The truth is He has already offered to carry all of it, so we may as well let Him.

The answer for overcoming the problem of where to start was embarrassingly obvious. You see, the concept God had placed on my heart to write about fifteen long years prior was one rooted in Psalm 119:105: "Your word is a lamp for my feet, a light on my path." The title of the book was to be *A Path Illuminated*, and the message was a reminder that God's Word often provides only a lamp's worth of light on our paths and that we must be willing to walk our paths one step at a time while trusting that His lamp will illuminate our next step once we act in faith.

This concept had been simmering in the back of my mind

for well over a decade, yet it still was not immediately obvious that the lesson applied to me as much as it did anyone. I had to take the first step. I had to do the first thing. I had to step out and finally choose obedience.

Yes, I had doubt. Yes, I felt clueless about where to start. And yes, I was called to start anyway. So, finally, I did. On April 19, 2015, I made a covenant with God that He owned the first hour of my day (an hour that had previously been the last hour of my sleep) every day Monday to Saturday for as long as it took to complete the task He had assigned to me so long before. I began the next day, and while that book still has not been published, you would not be holding this one if God's grace had not allowed me to take that first critical step.

Are you in possession of a call from God? Have you been hearing Him call your name and beckon you into a specific act of obedience? Are you doubting His call or your ability to answer it? Are you lost about where to start?

I offer you this basic advice: simply take the first step. Leave it to the Famous One to determine where He will lead you in the end. But I beg of you to delay no longer. He wants to use you in big ways, and in small, to glorify His name and elevate His fame. Enlist in His service and for that purpose. Take the first step. You will not regret it.

LET THE HERALD RUN

I love to read weighty books that force me to slow down and think. I love to be challenged by them and even forced to set a book aside momentarily to search out an understanding of what the author is trying to communicate. I appreciate it when an author stretches the bounds of my comprehension. But I am in the process of learning that God's nearness to me was first realized in easily palatable stories. God's fame, while awesome and vast in size, is typically first embraced through still, small, easily understood whispers of assurance that He is near.

As we think about how to be catalysts for the fame of God, we would do well to learn from God's instruction to Habakkuk, "Write down the revelation and make it plain on tablets so that a herald may run with it" (Hab. 2:2).

There is a place for challenging ourselves and fellow believers to explore more deeply into the profound mysteries of our God. It is a crucial place, and one in which each of us desperately needs to be pressing further. It is essential to our growth.

But when it comes to introducing the created to the Creator, the simple message of salvation should be made plain. Not ordinary, because there is nothing ordinary about the sacrifice that was made, and there would be no value in it if it were only ordinary. But despite its breathtaking value, it was—and is—a straightforward, simple, and free gift. It is a message we should take care to record in an easily digestible fashion. It should be recorded in a way that does not require any one person to deliver it. It should be done in a way that affords a herald—or anyone else for that matter—the ability to deliver it to its final destination.

CARRY THE FREIGHT

The victory formation is every football coach's favorite call to make. It happens when the game has been won and all that remains is to let the clock expire. The victory formation is the moment in which the outcome is acknowledged and celebrated. But it is not when the victory is actually achieved. It is not the portion of the game in which that outcome is determined.

In many cases, the final determinative plays of a game occur when the running back "carries the freight." This happens when the team with the lead has possession of the ball and simply needs to hold onto it long enough to pick up a first down while the clock is running. In order to keep the clock running, the offense will refrain from throwing passes and rely solely on the running back to carry the ball on each play. There is no deception—every fan in the stadium and everyone watching on TV knows what is coming. Even without an element of surprise, the running back is tasked with one job: carrying the freight. It is his job to get the football from where it is to where it needs to go without fumbling it. It is a simple task but not an easy one.

It is not at all unlike our job. God's fame is present. It is on the horizon. It is destined to reach and impact our culture, and the Enemy knows it. The opposition knows what is required to move it from where it is to where it will make an impact. The Enemy knows that we are its mode of transportation—that we are the ones charged with carrying the freight—and he will go to great lengths to stop us! So while our job is simple and straight-forward, it will not always be easy, and there will frequently be stiff opposition.

But my friends, the initial questions are simple ones. Are we on that wall? Have we stepped into the line of duty? Are we prepared to carry the freight?

There is no doubt that the needs of our culture are vast. There are many who can describe them. Let us not simply add to the number of those who can point out the problem. Let us be the ones who move toward the solution by carrying the magnificent fame of our God and all its healing and restorative power into the culture.

Let us carry the freight to a place where the victory formation can be called!

PART III

. . . . .

THE KNOWLEDGE

I stand in awe of your deeds, Lord.
—HABAKKUK 3:2

CHAPTER 9

. . . .

REMEMBER TO UNDERSTAND

Come near to God and he
will come near to you.
—JAMES 4:8

I still remember the awe I felt the first time I saw the ocean. Dad and Mom loaded my siblings and me into our van, and we made the long drive from central Illinois to the beaches of Florida. Our destination was Panama City Beach, and it was the first time any of my siblings or I had seen the ocean. Looking back, it is clear to me that we underestimated the awe it would inspire and were taken aback by its incredible vastness.

We had, of course, seen pictures of the ocean, and even studied many aspects of it. We had an academic understanding of what to expect, and as we neared our destination, we got glimpses from the highway of the Atlantic between the buildings. But when we pulled in to the beachfront hotel and piled out of the van to scramble around to the beach side of the hotel, textbooks and partial glimpses were overwhelmed in an instant by sheer reality.

It was one of those moments where all your senses go into overdrive. I remember how beautiful it was and how distinctly the air smelled like salt. But what I remember most specifically is the incredible power it possessed. I was stunned by the vastness of what I could see, but what surprised me was how much of the power I could actually *feel*—even before stepping foot in it. The size, motion, and energy of this incredible body of water could literally be felt as I rounded the corner of the hotel.

I am pretty sure my siblings were experiencing the same feelings, because all of us went immediately into the water—fully clothed. I would be remiss if I did not compliment my parents on their willingness to endure the inconvenience of letting us enjoy the experience in this nonconventional way. It would have been so much easier for us to first check in to our hotel and get changed into our swimming gear. But that would have dulled the impression of our first brush with the ocean. Instead, in one moment we caught our first glimpse, and in the next we immersed ourselves in it.

In those few moments, our knowledge of the ocean became firsthand and personal, and the awe we had been told we should feel for it became genuine. It was no longer an academic awe but rather an experienced one—and dare I say, an authentic one.

We were in awe not because we had been told, but because we had seen and we had touched. We knew for ourselves. We were convinced, and therefore our awe was real.

When Habakkuk professed his awe for God's mighty deeds, he still had not experienced them. He was still speaking in faith about what his God would do, and he was doing so even though he knew there was still great turmoil to come. Habakkuk had not yet seen or felt God's mighty deeds, but his faith and his stepping into action caused him to be convinced of them.

How do I know he was convinced?

I know because we are not truly awed by things of which we are not convinced. We are not moved into action by things we believe to be fraudulent. We are awed and moved to action by things of which we are absolutely convinced to be genuine and in which we place great value. Habakkuk was in awe. He had become convinced. He was confident and sure about the identity of his God, and about the power He possessed.

If we are to be equally awed and convinced, our belief in what we know to be true about God will need deep roots. The character and the Word of our God will need to be deeply ingrained in our spirits. If we want to see Him move—and if we want to be a part of that move—we must pursue a deeply intimate knowledge of Him. We must be absolutely fixated on who He is, on what He has said, and on what He is still saying.

A genuine awe of and conviction about the beauty and power of the ocean requires a firsthand encounter.

A genuine awe of and conviction about the beauty and power of our God also requires a firsthand encounter. It requires the pursuit of an ever-deeper knowledge. It requires that we remember to understand.

THE FOUNDATION OF FAME

We have been called to carry and proclaim God's fame into all the land. In order to carry out this duty, we must first possess His fame. We must first understand who He is. If we forget God's mighty acts, we cannot fully grasp His ways. But to actually possess His fame, we must do more than simply remember or recall the things He has done. We must also dedicate ourselves to an ever-greater understanding of Him. That knowledge will form the foundation of our ability to carry His fame.

In Matthew 1:23, we find the recitation of a prophecy originally found in Isaiah 7:14: "The virgin will conceive and give birth to a son, and they will call him Immanuel (which means 'God with us')." Before the salvation story of Jesus ever played out, God was expressing His desire to be with us. The very reason He sent His only son to die for us was His desire to be in proximity with us—the pinnacle of His creation.

While it is certainly true that God desires His fame to be known throughout the land, His desire for His relationship with us is to know and be known. He desires our commitment to learning His ways in great detail, in order that we might draw closer to His intimate knowledge of us, which is drawn from His having created us. He already fully knows, but He yearns to be more fully known, and He has asked us to pursue Him in that way.

Fortunately, in what can only be described as the most generous of acts, the God of the universe has promised that this will not be an elusive pursuit. So many times, we pursue things without any guarantee we can obtain them. Whether it is an educational degree, a job promotion, or a business endeavor, we regularly embark on pursuits without any assurance of the final outcome.

Not so with God's plea that we search Him out! His Word is replete with assurances that if we will demonstrate a desire to know Him, He will make Himself known. If we show up to converse, He will meet us in that place.

Consider Matthew 7:7–8: "Ask and it will be given to you; seek and you will find; knock and the door will be opened to you. For everyone who asks receives; the one who seeks finds; and to the one who knocks, the door will be opened."

It *will* be given.

You *will* find.

The door *will* be opened.

Those are promises. They are certainties. They are not elusive. But while the presence of God in our life is offered unconditionally, it is not offered automatically. There is a relationship role we must play.

Ask.

Seek.

Knock.

The God of the universe wants to draw near, but He will only do so if He is an invited guest. He will not force His way in. You see, His deepest desire is not so different from one with which we can relate: He longs to be pursued. He wants to be desired. He is asking to be the object of our affection.

In my book *In Search of the King*,[1] I wrote extensively about Jeremiah 29:13, "You will seek me and find me when you seek me with all your heart." It is probably my second-favorite assurance in Scripture that our pursuit of God will not go unanswered. My favorite assurance of this occurs in the very next verse, Jeremiah 29:14: "'I will be found by you,' declares the LORD."

My friends, He is eager to be found and eager to draw near

to us. But He desires that we seek Him out. He has asked that we yearn to understand His ways.

You should understand, however, that this pursuit comes with a word of warning. While there is obviously great benefit from attaining a deeper knowledge of God and His ways, there is also a great price to pay for failing to search out His wonders. Although primarily focused on commands pertaining to the Sabbath, Hebrews 4:1 suggests the possibility of others perishing as a result of following our disobedience. It is sobering to think that my failure to understand might lead others astray, but it is certainly true. Our actions influence the choices that others make. If we fail to fully understand God's ways and choose instead to lean on our own understanding, there will be many who suffer the consequences. It leads me to ask, "How committed am I to knowing the face of God in order that others do not miss out on all that God has in store for them?" The stakes are high, and those who are affected by our choices are great in number.

The gift of salvation is free and readily available. The entrance into relationship with God is open to all and without barrier of entry. But to access His fame, we must take the next step. We must dedicate ourselves to understanding His ways. We must remember to understand.

DRAWING NEAR

Why are we so frequently hesitant to draw near to God or to run to Him with our challenges? Why is it that we profess to want more proximity with Him and know that He has promised to answer our call (Jer. 33:3), yet we do not even take the easy and obvious steps to draw near to Him? Why is it that we feel unsure about how to convincingly invite others into relationship with their Creator?

The only logical answer to these questions is that we are not fully convinced of the cross. It sounds outlandish and offensive to even say it, but is there really any other reasonable explanation? If you and I are genuinely and thoroughly convinced that the Son of God came down to earth in human form in order to save us, would we still be hesitant? If we believed in an unqualified way that Jesus willingly carried a Roman cross down the Via Delarosa to die a painful death as payment for our sin, would it even be possible to respond in any way other than rushing to His side and shouting for others to join us?

I do not think there is another answer. I think the reason we wait, and the reason we refrain from sharing with the world, is that our fear of being wrong still outweighs our conviction that we are correct. We think that Jesus is who He says He is. We think it with enough conviction to say it out loud. But we are not absolutely convinced. We are not convinced to the point where our reputation is of no regard to us when weighed against the urgency of being in His presence and inviting others into it as well.

My friends, I ask these questions not that we might feel shame over having doubt. Quite the contrary! I ask these questions because they represent a nearly universal challenge to our belief, and they hold the key to unleashing the promise we have been discussing in these pages—the promise of immersing ourselves in His fame.

If we are going to be used by Him in a mighty way, we will have to become convinced.

If we want to rest in Him, we have to run to Him with our burdens (Matt. 11:28).

If we want Him to come near to us, we must act on His instructions to come near to Him (James 4:8).

I know well that it is far easier to get excited about the things God will do in and through us than it is to pursue a deeper knowledge and understanding of His ways. The first sounds like it is part of an epic story (it is), while the latter sounds like a tedious chore. Truthfully, while a pursuit of God's ways is often gloriously refreshing and always highly worth it, there is also certainly a sacrificial element to it. There is absolutely a requirement that we lay down our personal desires and pursuits in exchange for prioritizing the pursuits of God. In the beginning, those sacrifices can feel every bit like a chore.

But remember, our aim is not what occurs in the beginning. Our aim is to prepare ourselves for an eternity with our Maker. Our aim is to improve our proximity with Him now so that we might know Him better and more effectively convince others to be in proximity with Him alongside us. If that is our true aim, the sacrifice required is barely a consideration at all.

DRAW OTHERS NEAR

Dr. Dick Foth is a self-described "grandfather figure" for our church. The description does not really fit if it is being applied to Dr. Foth's energy or zeal for life and teaching—both are overflowing with the joy and vigor of youth. But the description aptly defines the role he has played in Pastor Mark's life and the authority and expertise he provides for all of us who get to hear from him periodically. When Dr. Foth speaks, I listen. I listen because I know his track record with me. I know how his proximity to the Father translates into messages that pierce my heart, convict me of wrongdoing, and inspire me into deeper relationship.

To put it simply, Dr. Foth is accomplished in the art of drawing others to join him in drawing near to God. It is not an accident he is good at it, but rather a by-product of his intentionality to make the message of the gospel palatable.

Dr. Foth recently reminded us that the Bible was originally void of chapters and verses. It was all long form, with no divisions for ease of reading. Chapter divisions were not added until the thirteenth century, and verses were not included until the sixteenth century. How remarkable is that? More than fifteen hundred years after Jesus walked the earth, His followers were still taking tangible steps to make His message more palatable and accessible! In all reality, that work continues even today. Because of technological advances, the Bible has reached more of the globe than ever before. Many of us carry the entire Bible on smartphones in our pockets.

Access to the Word of God is easier in more parts of the world than ever before. But, of course, having access to something is not the same as understanding how it can impact your life. That job now falls to us. A deeper knowledge of Him should be naturally followed by a desire to make it easier for others to access and know Him. To say it another way, His fame will more rapidly expand if we carry on the tradition of finding ways to make His name and fame more accessible and palatable for others.

Of course this does not give us liberty to add or subtract from the gospel. The reality is that the gospel invitation includes both sacrifice and resurrection. We cannot diminish the sacrificial side of following Jesus without destroying the core of the message. But we certainly can, and should, look for ways to present the gospel story in ways that will reach the hearts of people. The decision of what to do with the message rests with each of them, and many will reject it because of the sacrifice involved. But that does not change or diminish our responsibility to skillfully present them with a choice and to do it in a way that fully shows off the splendor of all He has offered us.

We draw near to God in order that He might draw near to us. That proximity affords us understanding about how to draw others to Him as well. That understanding comes with responsibility, including the task of using our God-given creativity to present His story in ways that are as unique as His character.

Be as creative as your Creator.

Draw near to Him in order that He may draw near to you.

Let the unique message of your life draw others to Him in a way that is equally unique.

But first, remember to understand.

CHAPTER 10

. . . .

WHO KNOWS MY NAME?

A good name is more desirable
than great riches;
to be esteemed is better than silver or gold.

—PROVERBS 22:1

There is a crisis of loneliness among the most famous people in the world. It seems impossible, because famous people are by definition surrounded and seen by many other people. We can understand if they suffer from any number of other afflictions or challenges, but surely loneliness should not be among them. And yet, it is fairly common to hear a superstar profess something along the lines of what actress Claire Danes said recently: "Fame doesn't end loneliness."[1]

How can this possibly be? We think of loneliness as separation from everyone else and fame as being the object of everyone else's attention. In reality, both of those assumptions are wrong. Loneliness stems not from a place of being physically alone but from a lack of being truly known. It is a feeling of facing our challenges and struggles without the assistance of others who love us. Quite frankly, unless we are intentional about staying rooted where we are really and truly known, it is a place we are even more vulnerable to land as our name becomes known to the masses.

As a result, we should not be shocked when the famous grapple with loneliness. Rather, I am confident it is one of the most difficult pitfalls for them to avoid. We are wired to be known intimately by a few, but the limelight of our culture pushes public figures to a place where it becomes impossible for them to separate themselves from their own fame. Their overwhelming fame smothers any depth of relationship they either had previously or attempt to cultivate after achieving fame.

The famous have pursued and achieved a wide breadth of fame, and yet many still feel alone. The reason is simple. We are designed to be known deeply rather than broadly. That is not to say that we should not be known broadly, as well, evidenced by promises made to Abraham, Joshua, and others, but we were first created to be intimately known by our Creator, and any broader fame must be born out of that secure place if it is to have any value or staying power.

Breadth of fame without depth of fame is a recipe for loneliness.

WHERE AM I FAMOUS?

Who knows my name? Where am I famous? Similarly, who do I want to know my name, and in what ways do I desire to be famous? The answers to these questions reveal a lot about our priorities. They are also great indicators of how well I am avoiding the trap of pursuing breadth of fame rather than depth of fame—or perhaps the adulation of the masses rather than intimacy with the Creator and those who know me best.

Pastor Mark often speaks and writes about the fact that one of his greatest life goals is to be famous in his own home. At first blush, that feels obvious, because the members of our families should be the most important people in our lives. But the layer that makes this difficult is the fact that they also know us best. To be famous in your home requires a mutual atmosphere of authenticity and forgiveness. It requires an embrace of the unlovely along with the lovely.

I am a sinner. It is, of course, an obvious admission, but most of you reading this book only know it in a general sense. You know I am a sinner because all have sinned and fallen short of the glory of God (Rom. 3:23). You know I am a sinner, but you do not know which sins afflict me the deepest. You do not personally experience the struggle or the consequence of my shortcomings. You have a general knowledge of the fact I am flawed, but most of you are essentially free of any known consequence stemming from those flaws.

My friends, colleagues, and acquaintances are a bit closer to those consequences. They have more evidence of my defects and suffer more significantly from my shortcomings. The impact of my sinful nature is a bit greater at this level, as any fallout from my sin can have a trickle-down effect on them and their daily environment.

But my wife, Brooke, feels something close to the full weight of my sinful nature. Brooke has a greater awareness of my fallen state than anyone on the planet, and endures a greater share of the consequence of that sin than anyone. It is one reason that marriage is a difficult endeavor, because in order to achieve the spiritual intimacy a marriage needs, our spouses are necessarily exposed to the muck of our sin in the process. This reality is expressed in the traditional wedding vows when the couple promises to stand by each other "for better, for worse." Our spouses see our best traits up close and personal, and they deal with our greatest weaknesses up close and personal as well.

It is a scary proposition, but it is also what gives the marriage relationship so much value. Yes, I am a sinner. Brooke is deeply aware of it. Yet she loves me unconditionally. Brooke is a sinner, as well. I am deeply aware of it. Yet I love her unconditionally. The truth is that our love is deep not despite our mutually known flaws but because of them. It is easy to love the lovely side of any person. Who doesn't want to enjoy the beautiful, fun, caring side of someone? Candidly, that is not difficult, nor is it particularly valuable. It is infinitely more valuable and comforting to be loved by someone who knows and accepts your weaknesses. That is what gives the marriage relationship strength and what affords it the ability to impact the world on a deeper level.

Yes, the value of my relationship with Brooke is found partially in what we add to each other. But that value pales in comparison to the value that comes from being fully known—warts, sin, and all—and fully loved anyway.

I suggest a mastery of this pursuit begins with the question, Do we live our lives in a genuine enough way for the people who know us best to think the most highly of us? This is not achieved by hiding our sins from the world. In fact, the opposite is true. Our goal must be for the people who know us when our best face is not on and when our best foot is not forward, to still see some-one who is pursuing the almighty God with everything we have. Our pursuit should be less about how many know our names and more about ensuring that those who do know them also know the Name above all names as a result of it.

That pursuit begins in our homes.

Am I famous in my home?

Are you famous in your home?

Is the Famous One famous in your home?

A FATHER'S NAME FOR US

The name you were given at birth is a defining feature of your story. It carries with it the mark of the family you were born into and the reputation that precedes you into the world. This name is your first identity.

The other names you are called have the potential to shape the way you look at the world. Nicknames, titles, teams or groups you are a part of, and attributes that are spoken of you all have the power to either spur you on beyond yourself or deliver a blow of defeat that stops you in your tracks.

But it is the name (or names) our Father in heaven gives us that says the most about us. It is not so different from the impact that is felt through what our human fathers say of us. A father's duty is to protect, provide, and nurture. My first instinct is to think about these duties in a purely physical sense. For example, I must protect my children from harm, provide them with food, clothing, and shelter, and nurture them into a deeper knowledge of both their God and the world around them. But it is abundantly clear that these duties go well beyond the physical. They extend into every component of our children's lives.

A father has a disproportionate impact on the level to which a child is protected from mental, spiritual, or relational harm in the world. A father has a duty to provide resources and structure through which a child can follow the example of Jesus and grow "in wisdom and stature, and in favor with God and man" (Luke 2:52). A father has a responsibility to nurture the natural gifts and the intrinsic motivations of his children. These are sacred duties, and they are at the very foundation of fatherhood.

But in my experience it is the identities a father speaks over his children that make the most difference. It is the things a father speaks over and about his children that have the greatest—and longest lasting—impact on who they become. When a father says to his child, "You are special," or, "You are strong," or, "You were made for a purpose," it does more than just communicate a fortifying and inspiring message. It also communicates that the child's identity is valued by the one for whom he or she is named. It does not simply bestow belonging; it locates that belonging squarely within the confines, strength, and identity of their father. Research is beginning to confirm this fact that we have long known by instinct—a father's words over us have disproportionate impact and value. This is true in both positive and negative ways.

I know this to be true in the lives of my own children. The words and the names I speak over Jude, Brell, and Hope have the power to move them to action or paralyze them. My affirmation is constantly desired, and my rebuke is extremely sobering to them. By the way, this is true of Brooke's words over them as well. Brooke has more impact on the identity and character of our kids than anyone in the world. She is their primary caretaker, nurturer, educator, and mentor. She is the one with whom they spend the most time, and her words over them are every bit as critical. But a father's words are critical in a slightly different way. A mother's words protect, provide, and nurture in a way that is very often tangible. The impact of a father's words might often seem less tangible, but they carry with them the power of identity.

I have given each of my kids a defining word for their lives at this stage. It is certain that other words will be added over time, and even possible that the defining word for each of them may change, evolve, or mature over time. But the point is a simple one: I want to call out the positive traits I see in them, using the words I speak over them.

My word for Jude is *story*. Jude has always had a passion for stories. He loves books, movies, plays, bedtime stories, or anything else with a plot. He loves listening to or watching stories, and he loves telling stories. He has a gift for noticing the importance of subtle plot lines or emotional components of stories, and I believe that gift will play an important role in the stories Jude will tell the world. I have told Jude that he is a part of the greatest story ever told, and that his gift for story is one that God will no doubt incorporate into His story.

Brell's word is *love*. Brell has this uncanny gift for noticing others. It is inherited from Brooke, as each of them will notice and care for the need of another before I ever even lift my eyes from the task at hand. Brell is drawn to acts of genuine service and takes real joy in showing love through practical action. I tell her that this kind of love can be hard to find in this world and that part of her mission will be to show others that it still exists and that it points to her Jesus.

Hope's word is *sing*. If you know Hope, then you have heard her sing! With the possible exception of a few minutes worth of shyness upon first meeting, Hope is nearly always singing. It is her preferred method of communication and sometimes her only method for a long period of time. She is constantly humming, and there is not a show tune that fails to get her up and dancing. I tell Hope that her gift for song will show the world what it means for the praise of God to be continually on our lips.

These words have become part of the fabric of our kids' identities. Jude knows he has the gift of story. Brell knows she is a unique expression of God's love. Hope understands that singing is a way she can spread joy. These attributes have become part of the names—and the identities—spoken over our kids by their father. The profession of these words carries real power.

Your heavenly Father knows *your* name, as well. In fact, He calls you by name and claims you for Himself (Isa. 43:1). He knows your shortcomings, but He also knows your giftings, because it was He who put them in you!

A NAME FOR YOU

Of course, words from a father can also have the opposite effect. Words can tear down and destroy a sense of identity. Often worst of all, the absence of any words at all from a father can leave a void that communicates abandonment or loneliness in the midst of an intimidating world. I am painfully aware of how many of you are reading this chapter from a place of either no relationship or a broken relationship with your earthly father. For you, this message has the potential to tear you down rather than inspire you.

The good news is that your heavenly Father anticipated the gaps that would emerge as a result of empowering human beings with the mantle of fatherhood. He anticipated the failure and the weakness that would inevitably be displayed and the precious children who would not experience an earthly father who speaks words of identity over them. He anticipated that you would be inclined to speak words of desperation about yourself as a result of this difficult circumstance. He anticipated it, and He stepped in to provide a divine replacement for you.

You may not have words of identity from a human father to which you can hold. But the Creator of both the universe and your being has been speaking your name since the beginning of time! The Enemy may have planted false suggestions that you are without association, identity, or value, but your Father has rebuked that with the words of truth He has been speaking over you.

You feel unnoticed. He says, "I see you" (Gen. 16:13).

You feel attacked. He says, "I will rescue you" (Ps. 72:12–14).

You feel discarded. He says, "You are mine; I have called you by name" (Isa. 43:1).

You feel alone. He says, "Come to me" (Matt. 11:28).

You feel besieged. He says, "I will preserve you" (Ps. 32:7).

You feel void of purpose. He says, "You are called" (Isa. 42:6).

You have been wronged. He says, "I will restore you" (1 Peter 5:10).

You mourn the absence of family. He says, "You are my child" (2 Cor. 6:18).

You feel stained with sin. He says, "You are precious in my sight" (Isa. 43:4).

You feel unlovely. He says, "You are my delight" (Isa. 42:1).

You feel unworthy. He says, "I gave it all just to be with you" (Rom. 8:32).

My friends, earthly fathers have been given the special gift of an outsized role in their children's lives. But the presence of a positive earthly father does not determine whether or not we belong to the eternal heavenly Father.

Who knows your name? He knows your name.

He knows your name because He gave it to you.

He knows your name because it is His name.

You are His child.

You belong to Him.

CHAPTER 11

INVEST IN THE OLD MAN

Even when I am old and gray,
do not forsake me, my God,
till I declare your power to the next generation,
your mighty acts to all who are to come.

—PSALM 71:18

When a person is on his or her deathbed, he or she tends to see the priorities of life on earth more clearly and accurately than ever before. We have all heard the stories about a dying man who regrets having worked so hard instead of really investing in his wife and children. Or the dying woman who suddenly realizes she never actually pursued her dreams. There is something about approaching the end of our lives that causes us to become acutely aware of what our priorities should have been. As the burdens and the stresses of meeting earthly obligations begin to fade away, we are left contemplating whether we spent time on the things that mattered most.

The inescapable truth is that life is very short. James calls it a vapor or a mist that appears for a short time and then vanishes (James 4:14). We know intellectually this is true, and we even recognize many of the things for which our dying selves will want our lives to have been spent. But I, for one, still find it difficult to live daily in a way that focuses on these eternal priorities without getting bogged down in the urgencies of the here and now. I desire to look back on my life with contentment rather than regret, but that calibration can be hard to grasp in the midst of a daily grind.

So how do we accomplish it? How do we reorient our priorities now in order to look back with satisfaction on lives applied to the things we will recognize in hindsight as being the most important? How do we avoid the regret of pouring ourselves out for things that will simply vanish with the mist?

I have found it helpful to turn the question on its head. Rather than thinking only about what I will regret from my deathbed, it is helpful to try to identify what I will look back on with satisfaction. What are the things I can set my hands to now that will give me assurance in that moment? What are the endeavors that will fill my weakening mind with peace and fulfillment rather than disappointment and regret?

As we attempt to answer these questions, ask yourself, "What will the old man (or woman) version of me be like?" When most of your life is in the rearview mirror, what will the bits and pieces combine to create? Will the people and the things you have invested in result in a person worth being? Are you living in a way that is greater than the present moment's fulfillment? Is there a longer-lasting impact that is guiding your decisions?

The God-directed answers to these questions will help us have an impact during every season of our lives. They will focus our efforts today, but they will also build value in our characters so that we might still bear fruit in our older age (Ps. 92:12–14). It is tempting to live only for today even as it relates to proclaiming God's fame. But if we can learn to think through a lens of investing—through deposits of character building—in the persons we will be during our later years, it will make the old-age version of ourselves overflow with internal wisdom that can be offered as our physical abilities wane. It will ensure we do not forfeit the rich value and purpose that exists in those years of our lives.

So how do we shift from a perspective of prioritizing who we are now to one of investing in the persons we will be in the end? The most significant factor in achieving this mind-set is a cementing of the Word and an ironclad conviction that the holy God lives in and moves through us. If we have a deep assurance of these realities, we are free to choose to invest in the old man or woman version of ourselves. We are liberated from the insatiable temptation to live only in the urgency of the here and now.

EXPERIENCE IS GLORY

Proverbs 20:29 says, "The glory of young men is their strength, gray hair the splendor of the old." So much of the human experience is contained in that one sentence. Our natural tendency is to spend our youth chasing things we know will be gone soon—sooner than we can imagine! We obsess over our weight, our fitness, and our physical appearance in general. We focus, or "glory in," how we are viewed by the public. We drive ourselves to ward off the physical effects of aging we know are coming. Death and taxes are spoken of as the only certain things in life, but we spend plenty of time trying to avoid both.

The point is that the glories of youth are often spent on physical pursuits. I am no exception. While I have never been mistaken for one who spends his time at Muscle Beach (I have been tall and skinny since I was a freshman in high school), I look back now with fascination on how much joy I found in physical pursuits. I longed for and often found positive results by exercising the strength of my youth. Baseball, basketball, running, working out, and eventually triathlons were the activities to which I applied myself, but I can see now that I was primarily seeking to enjoy the vigor of youth.

There is nothing inherently wrong with youth and the strength that comes with it. In fact, youthful strength is absolutely necessary for motivating and propelling many of the actions that are needed to build a livelihood. It is also one of the primary ways the younger generation can serve the older. Strength and vigor are God-given and if done properly are rightly gloried in.

But youth does not last. It is here for a time, and then it fades. Yes, it is true that fitness can and should be maintained, but even the most diligent and faithful will concede that physical fitness is easier to attain and maintain in our twenties than it is in our sixties and seventies. While God has set eternity in our hearts, we are each still appointed a time to be born and a time to die (Eccl. 3). None of us will escape it. So while the glories of our youth are a gift, there is a danger in giving them too much focus.

If we are glorying only in the strength of our youth, what will we draw on when our youth is gone?

The good news is that while our youth fades away, it can be replaced by something even better if we allow it. When Proverbs speaks of gray hair being the splendor of the old, it is signifying the shift that occurs in the primary gift we have to offer the world. In our youth, it is strength; in our later years, it is wisdom born out of experience. It is knowledge of what life's twists and turns look like that can be offered to those walking behind us, and it has the potential to be far more valuable than the strength of our youth it is replacing.

This is not a call to reject the joys of youth. Far from it! But it is a call to set our affection on pursuits that can be carried throughout our entire lives. It is a call to recognize the changes in what we have to offer the world as our seasons of life change and to focus our investments on things that will enrich all those seasons rather than just the fleeting season of our youth.

If you are currently in the later years of life, and the glory of your youthful strength is but a memory, are you being intentional about sharing the wisdom of your experience with those whose hair is not yet gray? Do you recognize the rich value that comes with all that you have experienced, or are you holding it in because you are still glorying in your youth that has since faded? I challenge you to take an honest look at your perspective, because if you will decide to share from that wisdom, you will find that you have more to offer the world from your wisdom than you ever had to offer it from your strength.

If you are still in your youth, are you mindful of the fact that your youth will fade? Are you remembering to invest in the person you will be long after your strength has faded? Are you mindful that your youth is a wonderful gift for a time, but your investments into the old-age version of you are what will reap the longest-lasting fruit?

Who will the old man or old woman version of you be? What do you want that version of you to draw from as you relate to the world around you? How can you adjust your efforts now to ensure your investments are not lost along with the strength of your youth?

This should be an exhilarating proposition, because the very best gift we have to offer the world is an intimate familiarity with the most high God. If we will commit to invest daily in that relationship, we will build up a deep reservoir of wisdom and value that can be drawn on throughout our lives. Our gray hair will be a sign that we are rich in experience, and our splendor will be found in sharing that experience with the young, who are seeking their own splendor.

So invest in the old man version of you. Invest in the old woman version of you. Seek out lasting experience and wisdom over things that fade. That is how splendor will be found and how His glory will be revealed in us.

REJOICE IN THE TRIAL

It is easy to let this world beat me down. I have a physical body that is designed not as an indestructible fortress but as a make-shift tent that will soon be blown away (2 Cor. 5:1). I have a sinful nature that is inclined not to what is pure but to what is destructive (Rom. 7:15–20). And I live in a world that is far from inclined toward what is right and just, but rather one that is desperately devoted to the depraved (Rom. 3:9–19).

Because of these factors, I am bound to experience suffering. I am certain to break down physically. I will absolutely lose heart from time to time. It is all part of being fully human. But we can overcome if our affections are set on His fame rather than our own. We can rise above the discomfort that occurs and persists if our spirits are rooted in the eternal that will come rather than the broken reality that is our present.

James described this struggle in a way that has become familiar to us, but his words are worth returning to regularly. As you read his exhortation to us, notice the timing and the focus of God's work in us. It does not occur after we survive the trial or the brokenness; it occurs in the midst of it. The intent of the trial is not primarily to build our external value; it is to fortify our internal strength.

> Consider it pure joy, my brothers and sisters, whenever you face trials of many kinds, because you know that the testing of your faith produces perseverance. Let perseverance finish its work so that you may be mature and complete, not lacking anything. If any of you lacks wisdom, you should ask God, who gives generously to all without finding fault, and it will be given to you. (James 1:2–5)

First, I have so often resisted this presentation of the timing of God's work in me. I have longed for, and asked Him for, a swift end to my struggles. I have done so out of a misguided belief that perseverance is simply some sort of divine endurance test. I have acted as though the only goal is to get to the other side of the struggle, at which point I will have passed the test. I have had it completely wrong, and there is a good chance you have as well!

Friends, we are not called to simply survive the struggle. The goal is to persevere through it. Perseverance means "to persist in a state, enterprise, or undertaking in spite of counter-influences, opposition, or discouragement."[1] We must persist! The value in the struggle is in the refusal to back down even when all seems lost. It is not in keeping our heads down and waiting for the storm to pass, but rather in raising our voices to the heavens and confronting God with the promises He has made to us.

It is not the finish line that produces the perseverance; it is the testing.

Do not wait until the storm has passed to rejoice. Rejoice in the midst of the storm, because it is the storm that God is using to build you up for what is to come.

Second, the focus of God's refining work in us will ultimately impact the world, but that is not its primary aim. The primary purpose for struggles that produce perseverance is an internal one. It is a strengthening and a refining of our spirits, the depths of which may never be known except to us. We are to let the work of perseverance run its course so that we might be internally mature and complete, lacking in nothing.

I do not think it is an accident that James tells us wisdom will be given freely if we simply ask, but the testing that produces perseverance has to run its course before we are complete. There is no shortcut. The ability to persevere is essential for the tasks we are being called to, but it takes time to accomplish its work. I am nearly always impatient and eager to ask God to simply move me through whatever it is I am facing. Yet in doing so, I forfeit the prize of perseverance. James put it beautifully this way: "Blessed is the one who perseveres under trial because, having stood the test, that person will receive the crown of life that the Lord has promised to those who love him" (James 1:12).

My friends, rejoice in the trial. Why? Not simply because it will one day be over. No, rejoice because persevering through it is an investment in the man or woman you will be on the other side. It is building the strength of your character and the value of who you will be in your old age.

TAKE HEART

This perseverance thing is not always—or even usually—easy. If you are like me, you will often feel like quitting. My heart wants to take on the struggle and confront the enemies of injustice and brokenness, but my body and my flesh often want to simply walk away. It is a constant struggle, and one I will not win on my own.

There are so many days when I lose heart. There are regularly long seasons where I feel as though I am physically wasting away in the struggle. In those moments, we would do well to remember Paul's words to the church at Corinth:

> All this is for your benefit, so that the grace that is reaching more and more people may cause thanksgiving to overflow to the glory of God. Therefore we do not lose heart. Though outwardly we are wasting away, yet inwardly we are being renewed day by day. For our light and momentary troubles are achieving for us an eternal glory that far outweighs them all. So we fix our eyes not on what is seen, but on what is unseen, since what is seen is temporary, but what is unseen is eternal. (2 Cor. 4:15–18)

The struggle is for our benefit, and it is for the glory and fame of God. Though our bodies may fail, we can be inwardly renewed day by day. An eternal glory is coming, and the work He is doing internally will last eternally.

Stay the course. Take heart. Persist through the struggle. Persevere. Invest in the old man. Invest in the old woman. Your crown is waiting on the other side.

CHAPTER 12

· · · · ·

EMBRACE THE POWER

*And these are but the outer
fringe of his works;
how faint the whisper we hear of him!
Who then can understand the
thunder of his power?*

—JOB 26:14

Brooke and I took the kids to a local animal farm not long ago. The farm is situated on federal land and benefits from views of the Potomac River. Given our family's love of the outdoors, it is a pretty ideal setting—water, trees, plants, hiking trails, and animals.

Brell (who was eight years old at the time) absolutely loves horses, so she was most excited to see the gorgeous horses at the riding stables nearby. Hope (then six years old) seemed most interested in the giant hogs wallowing in the mud. Jude (then ten years old) had a favorite that was a bit surprising. His interest was drawn to a chicken.

Jude's preference was not based on the type of animal but rather on the fact that this particular animal had escaped its enclosure. The chicken had managed to squeeze through a partially open gate and was running freely around the farm. As you might expect, this detail instantly grabbed Jude's interest, because now he could do more than just look *at* and talk *to* the animals. Now Jude could actually engage *with* one of the animals. Of course, by "engage with," I simply mean that Jude could chase it. That is just what boys (and let's face it, men) love to do— we chase things! It is natural and part of God's design. Certainly, we do not always harness this hard-wiring properly, but that does not invalidate the hard-wiring itself. We were made to chase, and God did not make a mistake when He designed us that way. He desired a creation that would pursue Him. And further, He needed a being that would pursue the rest of His creation.

So Jude chased the escaped chicken and, with the help of his sisters, actually even coaxed it back into its enclosure. It would be the only positive experience we had with enclosures that day.

Next to the chicken enclosure was a field with sheep. As we walked over to look at the sheep, Brooke and the kids were several feet in front of me. When they reached the edge of the field, Brooke leaned forward and grabbed the top of the fence, which, unbeknown to any of us, was electrified. The fence sent a jolt of electricity through her body and knocked her backward. Fortunately, the voltage was low and though Brooke was stunned and tingling for a good while, she was otherwise unhurt. The fence had done its job—it had rebuked and deterred Brooke without hurting her.

Looking back on it, we have had many good laughs about the visual image of Mom getting knocked backward by the fence, as well as the slight burning smell that followed her afterward. It was not funny at the time, but it sure is now! We have also laughed about the fact that the incident occurred immediately next to a sign that warned visitors to avoid touching the electrified fence. Our family loves to read, but we failed to show it that day.

TAKE HOLD OF THE POWER

Brooke should have been leery of that electrified line. She should have anticipated what would happen if she took hold of it, and opted to avoid it. And you know what? She would have done exactly that had she read the sign. Had she known about the power running through that fence, she would have been careful to avoid getting near it.

It is so very similar to how I treat God's power. I know it is real. I believe it is present in today's world. I understand it is capable of flowing through me. I recognize and profess its power. But I am afraid of it. I am afraid of it, and so I am careful to avoid getting too close to it. I am most certainly careful to avoid reaching out and taking hold of it. I am intrigued by the power, but even more than that, I am afraid of it rushing through me. So I stand back.

I think it is time we are honest with each other about the reasons we fear God's power being present in our lives. These reasons almost certainly vary person to person, but I think most of the reasons can be condensed into two main categories.

First, we are afraid of what we do not understand. Much like Habakkuk, we know of God's power by reputation only—or at least we think we know it by reputation only. We have heard about His mighty acts and the ways in which He has reached down to infuse His power into human situations. But those stories feel distant because God feels distant. Those stories feel like they are from a bygone era because we do not see them or hear about them in our lives today. Part of the reason for this is that we have failed to recognize His mighty acts, but more on that later. The bottom line is we do not have—or at least do not think we have—personal experience with His power. Therefore, we are bewildered by His power and afraid of it.

Second, we are afraid of the terrible side of God's power. I think this is the larger of our deterrents from embracing God's power. For you see, the most powerful forces in the world are both exhilarating and terrifying. Awesome and terrible. Life-giving and life-threatening. In order to release the positive attributes of these powers, one must also confront the imposing components of them. This is true for powers ranging from nature's weather patterns to human weapons of warfare. But the ultimate example of this phenomenon is the awesome and terrible fame of the almighty God.

Many of us claim to believe the power of God can overcome any obstacle and is the antidote for any number of societal ills. We profess and laud His power, and implore others to do the same. We utter words and sing songs calling for God's presence and intervention. If we truly believe what we say, then why do we not act on His promises and tap into His power? I suggest it is often because we are afraid of the terrible side of God's power. We do not understand how to take hold of the positive power while avoiding the wrathful side. We are afraid of getting knocked down by the surge of power.

We are also afraid of being set apart by the power. Imagine what would happen if God started using us in ways He used biblical heroes of faith. Imagine if the lame were healed, the deaf could hear, and the mute spoke in loud, clear voices. How would the world around us respond? I think there is a very good chance that a large percentage of the world would act as we have thus far—out of fear. I think much of God's power would be met with cynicism and criticism. I think the world around us would see their fear before they saw the benefits of God's power being present.

That would leave us set apart as a result of having embraced the power, and we are afraid of that possibility. We want to be set apart so long as it means being preserved for greatness. But when being set apart means risking alienation over association with His fame, we are less certain. We would rather fit in with those around us. If embracing the power of God will make us different from the world—and we sense that it will—we decide that maybe we will just steer clear for now.

It is time to be honest and come to grips with these fears. Because if we desire to see an awesome move of God's fame in our time—and I desperately do—we have to be willing to accept the danger that comes with it. The danger is what gives it power. If the power were weak—if the voltage were low—it would not be worth anything! If it were like the fence in our story, the only danger would be getting stunned by it. But because it is a power greater than any we have ever known, it has the capacity to destroy. So,

MY FAME, HIS FAME

in a sense, we are correct to be afraid of it. We are correct that an embrace of it will cost us much of what we are inclined to cling to. But it is time to channel that fear into motivation to handle the power correctly rather than letting fear cause us to abandon it altogether.

God's fame has been gathering for a while now. It is smoldering on the horizon and preparing to rush through the land. The time is near for His fame to be made known in personal ways. But it requires that I be willing to reach out and take hold of it. It requires that you overcome your fear and step forward to be a vessel through which the fame can course.

This world desperately needs the power to which we have access. But it is not a stagnant power. It is a rushing, coursing power, and it requires transport.

We are that transport. Will we reach out and take hold of it? Will we embrace it and ask God to use it through us? Or will our fear of being knocked off our feet cause us to turn and walk away?

The world watches and waits, because its fate hangs in the balance. It hangs on our decision. If the world this power was sent to save is to find rescue, we must embrace the power—both the awesome and the terrible.

AN EMPTY GODLINESS

My friend Bill Wichterman has a wonderful way of describing the type of influence to which he aspires. He says he cares less about the size and scope of his influence and more about its potency. To illustrate his point, he explains that the size of a container is far less important than what type of substance it contains.

For example, a small vial of a drug or radioactive substance is infinitely more potent than a vast container that is empty or filled with something benign.

Paul said it this way:

> But mark this: There will be terrible times in the last days. People will be lovers of themselves, lovers of money, boastful, proud, abusive, disobedient to their parents, ungrateful, unholy, without love, unforgiving, slanderous, without self-control, brutal, not lovers of the good, treacherous, rash, conceited, lovers of pleasure rather than lovers of God—having a form of godliness but denying its power. Have nothing to do with such people. (2 Tim. 3:1–5)

"Having a form of godliness but denying its power." I desperately want to avoid that statement being true about me! Paul warns that the last days will be filled with this kind of people, and it feels like that is coming to pass today. I feel the pull myself. It is so easy to become fixated on attaining a certain level of "godliness." I so naturally seek an appearance of "holiness." But to attain godliness or holiness of our own accord or in our own name is to wholly forsake the power of God.

How much better it would be—and how much more beneficial to both the world and ourselves— for us to lay aside the pursuit of a godly appearance (or any *appearance*, really) in favor of embracing a power of God that is beyond our control and aimed at something far greater than our own small reputations.

How much better it would be to stare down evil as a result of being unafraid than it is to cower in fear and avoid a confrontation. I do not want an empty form of godliness. I may be but a small vessel, but I want the substance that fills me to be potent. I want the courage to look evil in the eye and for both of us to realize that the power in me is greater than the power that is in it (1 John 4:4). That is the only way my life will be wholly given over to my God and to His fame.

THE BEST DEFENSE

The primary reason I want to fully embrace God's power is that He might do things beyond my wildest imagination. Actually, He has promised to do so. But I want to be one of the mechanisms by which His power is on display in my time. Mine is a proactive wish. I do not want to simply play defense against my own fleshly desires; I want to put points on the board for the eternal kingdom. I want to be on offense!

But there is a secondary reason, as well, and it is that a great offense is the best defense.

I am a Chicago Bears fan, but as anyone who has been following the NFL for the last couple of decades can tell you, it has been Tom Brady's world and everyone else is competing for second place. His New England Patriots have appeared in a whopping nine Super Bowls, winning six of them. The reasons for the franchise's success are many, but you will be hard-pressed to argue that Brady's constant brilliance as quarterback is not the most significant. He has amassed countless records along the way, but the most amazing attribute to me is the way in which he takes his game to another level in the fourth quarter when the outcome is on the line. This is especially true in the playoffs.

If Brady needs to score and gets the ball with even a few

seconds left on the clock in a playoff game, it seems as though he finds a way every time. If you want to beat the Patriots with Brady at the helm, you need to either find a way to take the lead as the clock expires or be so far ahead that the game is out of reach as the clock winds down—itself a near-impossible feat against Brady. Further, Brady most often converts these game-winning scores in a fashion that leaves no time on the clock for a counter-score. It is not as though the scores are always lightning fast. If his Patriots need a more methodical drive to seal the win at the end, Brady delivers it.

The Patriots have had some stellar defenses over the years as well, but in my opinion, their best defense has always been their Brady-led offense. If you do not let your opponents have the ball, it is much easier to keep them from scoring.

I have found this to be true in my own life as well. There are many opponents that can hinder the work of God's power in our lives—greed, lust, anger, jealousy, bitterness, just to name a few. But no matter the opponent, I have found the best defense against it is a strong offense. I find that it is easiest to resist the "shall nots" when I am consumed with a pursuit of the things He has called me to. I am the most insulated from and resistant to the things that would destroy me when I am the most committed to moving the proverbial ball down the field, and when I am setting my hand to tasks that are eternal.

In short, my best defense is a great offense.

We see several examples of this in Scripture, but perhaps the most familiar is King David with Bathsheba. The sins of David that get the most ink are his lust (2 Samuel 11:2: he saw Bathsheba bathing and desired her), his adultery (verse 4: he took action based on his lust), and his murder (verses 14–17: David had

Bathsheba's husband, Uriah, killed). But the scene for these sins was set in verse 1 when we learn that David should have been at war with his men, but he sent Joab in his place.

In short, David was not where he was supposed to be. David was not on offense. David was bored.

David's boredom and failure to be where he was supposed to be, doing what he was supposed to do, left him vulnerable. Obviously, his subsequent actions were entirely wrong in and of themselves, but I submit that the best time to play defense against those actions was not when he caught sight of a beautiful woman from the roof. No, the best time to play defense was far earlier. And the best way to play defense was to go on offense with the mission God had given him. Had David been on offense and carrying out the task God had assigned him, he would have never even been on that roof. He would have avoided the vulnerable state of being bored and burdened by a wandering eye. Instead of being drawn to give his strength for destruction, David would have been using his strength alongside his men and on behalf of his God.

Here is the reality: We cannot rely on a strong offense to avoid all temptation and danger. We have a sinful nature, and opportunities to engage that nature are going to present themselves. The allure of wealth. Your neighbor's bigger house or nicer car. Your friend's more rapid ascension up the career ladder. All these moments and more will occur, and we will need to resist. It is critical that we build defensive safeguards in our lives to get us through the temptations unscathed.

But so often these moments can be avoided altogether. We can often resist them simply by not being on the roof when we are supposed to be at war. We can avoid sending the defense back onto the field if we simply keep possession of the ball. We can avoid the pitfalls of sin by choosing instead to fully embrace and be fully immersed in the mighty power of God, the power that He will deploy when we are applying ourselves to the tasks for which He has commissioned us.

His power is intended to expand and go into all the land—yes!

But carrying that power and being on mission for it is also our best means of defense. It is the shield that surrounds us and protects us from the enemy (Ps. 3:3).

Do not be afraid. Reach out and embrace the power!

PART IV

· · · ·

THE REQUEST

Repeat them in our day,
in our time make them known;
in wrath remember mercy.

—HABAKKUK 3:2

CHAPTER 13

. . . .

DRY BONES

Very truly I tell you, whoever believes in me
will do the works I have been doing, and
they will do even greater things than these,
because I am going to the Father. And I will
do whatever you ask in my name, so that the
Father may be glorified in the Son. You may ask
me for anything in my name, and I will do it.
—JOHN 14:12–14

Habakkuk had moved from a place of doubt to a place of proclamation. He had professed his knowledge of what God had done in the past and stated his belief in what God could do in the present. In essence, Habakkuk had finally said, "I believe my God can do it."

But believing that our God is capable is not enough. Or at least it is not what He has asked of us as a prerequisite for unleashing His full presence and power. Yes, it is crucial that we believe He is able to do it. That belief sets the table for Him to arrive. It prepares the conditions and readies the atmosphere. *But it does not usher Him in.* For the full essence of God's power, fame, and presence to be realized, it often requires a request. It requires that those who have professed and proclaimed a belief take the additional step of actually inviting Him into their midst.

It requires God's people who have become accustomed to saying, "I believe my God can do it," to instead insist, "Do it again, God!"

This request is really at the core of our mission. When all else is stripped away, we were created and entrusted with a short time on earth so that we might insistently call forth and proclaim the fame of the mighty God. We are capable of acquiring knowledge and even designed to proclaim truth. But at the center of our purpose, we were created to seek after and carry His fame. We are the catalysts that move God's fame from something that is distant to something that is tangible. We are the way in which that fame is made real to those around us.

As I write and as you read, God's fame is gathering. It is smoldering on the horizon. It has the power to invade our culture, mend what is broken, heal the wounded, bridge the divides, restore the outcast, rescue the lost, and so much more. But that fame is waiting. It is waiting for a request. It is waiting for His people to call it out. It is searching for those of us who stand ready to be vessels and conduits of His fame.

The fame of God is ready to be poured out, but questions remain: Who will call it out? Who will live boldly expectant of a move of God, and step forward to be used by Him in a way that facilitates His fame? Who will make the request?

For Habakkuk, who longed for God's mighty fame and awesome deeds to again be present, the request was, "Repeat them in our day, in our time make them known; in wrath remember mercy" (3:2).

For you and for me, it might simply be, "Do it again, God!"

FLESH AND BONES

God's fame is real, but if we are honest, it often feels distant. If it feels distant to us—His people—how must it feel to those who do not know Him? If it often feels intangible to you and me, how will it be possible for the world to grasp the truth of His being? It seems like a herculean task to translate the fame of a transcendent God in a way that connects with a very tangible world. It is one thing to understand we are the vessels that bridge that divide, but it is another to take seriously the task of learning how to become the flesh-and-bones translation of His fame.

First, we have to be ready for a move of God's fame. That is really not even the best way to describe it, because God's fame is always on the move. It is always on the move, but most often it is not readily felt or experienced by the world around us unless and until we let it move through us.

God's fame is moving, but our neighbor is not embraced by His fame until we embrace them.

Injustice is not confronted by it until we confront it.

The hungry are not fed by it until we feed them.

The thirsty are not satisfied by it until we give them a drink.

The lonely are not befriended by it until we call them friend.

The ailing find no comfort in it until we carry the comfort to them.

The naked are not clothed by it until we clothe them.

Prisoners do not enjoy companionship with it until we visit them.

Please hear me. The fame of God is the answer to all these ills of society and humanity. But my friends, we—you and me—are the flesh and bones of God's fame. We—you and me—are what the world can physically see. We—you and me—are the hands and feet that allow those who most need God's fame to come into contact with it. We—you and me—are the way in which they can touch it, and by which they can take hold of it.

We have been asking, "What is mankind that you are mindful of them?" (Ps. 8:4). My friends, this is a huge part of that answer! Why is God so desperate for relationship with us? Yes, one reason is absolutely that he loves us with a sacrificial love beyond comprehension. But that is not the ultimate reason. No, the ultimate reason is always about pointing back to His glory and fame. He wants to bring glory unto Himself! He wants His creation to reflect His identity and bring honor to Him. And He has invested that desire within His creation—most notably the pinnacle of His creation, you and me. Why is God mindful of us? Because His glory is entangled with us!

So while I again ask, Who will call it out?, it might be even more important to ask ourselves, Are we moving and living in a way that reveals His fame? Are we the lens through which the fame of God can be seen? Are we putting ideas into action for the gathering fame of God to take on texture? Do our actions reflect an understanding of the reality that for God's fame to move from a shadowy, smoky vapor into something tangible with flesh and bones and connective tissue—into something that can be seen and touched, and that can tangibly impact our world—we have to join it?

We are the way that vapor becomes flesh and bones and has a real and tangible interaction with our world. We are the way it becomes more than a mist that cannot be gathered. And it is at the intersection of God's magnificent gathering fame and our simple and obedient move to action that our world comes face-to-face with the mighty power and fame of the one true God. If that does not give you a sense of purpose and exhilaration, nothing will.

Do you desire to have that kind of impact on the world? I certainly do, and it is absolutely within our grasp. In fact, it is the reason we were created. But if we want that type of influence, we have to move. We have to act. We have to become the flesh-and-bone vessels for His fame.

EZEKIEL'S ARMY

The decision to step forward into the line of duty and channel the fame of God may be made on an individual level, but it is anything but an individual pursuit. In fact, while there is a place in the ranks reserved for each of us, the true power of His fame is realized when it flows through a body of believers who are standing shoulder to shoulder with one another. That kind of fame constitutes a force against which no evil can stand, and it depends on each of us stepping up to fill our gap in the line. We are required to make an independent choice as individuals, but we rise and stand together as one. That is when the true force of God's fame is realized.

Ezekiel 37 gives us a Hollywood-worthy depiction of this concept:

> The hand of the LORD was on me, and he brought me out by the Spirit of the LORD and set me in the middle of a valley; it was full of bones. He led me back and forth among them, and I saw a great many bones on the floor of the valley, bones that were very dry. He asked me, "Son of man, can these bones live?"
>
> I said, "Sovereign LORD, you alone know."
>
> Then he said to me, "Prophesy to these bones and say to them, 'Dry bones, hear the word of the LORD! This is what the Sovereign LORD says to these bones: I will make breath enter you, and you will come to life. I will attach tendons to you and make flesh come upon you and cover you with skin; I will put breath in you, and you will come to life. Then you will know that I am the LORD.'"
>
> So I prophesied as I was commanded. And as I was prophesying, there was a noise, a rattling sound, and the bones came together, bone to bone. I looked, and tendons and flesh appeared on them and skin covered them, but there was no breath in them.
>
> Then he said to me, "Prophesy to the breath; prophesy, son of man, and say to it, 'This is what the Sovereign LORD says: Come, breath, from the four winds and breathe into these slain, that they may live.'" So I prophesied as he commanded me, and breath entered them; they came to life and stood up on their feet—a vast army. (Ezek. 37:1–10)

First, in so many ways, we—the individuals who make up the church of Jesus Christ—are dead. I do not mean that in a finger-pointing, self-loathing sort of way. In fact, I adore the church, along with the growing desire and increasing expressions of God's great love that I see pouring from today's church. I see a hunger for the things of God and a growing activation that is impacting the world in a way not seen before in my lifetime. I know from my work that this phenomenon is worldwide, and it thrills me to my core.

Even so, there is much more life available. There is much more power and wonder accessible to us, and it is evidenced from cover to cover throughout Scripture. While I see strong evidence of believers pursuing the things and the heart of God, I do not see nearly enough instances of His overwhelming presence showing up in ways that are undeniable to a world of unbelievers. I do not see the pillar of cloud and fire of Exodus that led the Israelites. I do not see the lame walking, the deaf hearing, the blind seeing, and the mute speaking in numbers I believe possible.

I realize I might have lost you with that last paragraph. There are many who like this idea of Jesus showing up in their lives until there is a suggestion that His power can do big and scary things. There are many who will be skeptical, and there are more who do not want anything to do with it. I have been in both of those camps for most of my life, but no more. Count me on the side of being desperate for it. Count me on the side of believing it is the only real hope for a world that was created to need the awesome power of its Creator. Count me on the side of wanting to witness this kind of awesome and tangible power in my day and in my presence. I want that power to cease being distant in terms of both time and experience. I am ready for it to occur today and firsthand.

In sum, I do not see nearly enough examples of God's fame being embodied in a way that compellingly draws the masses to it. My friend Scott Sauls wrote about this idea in his book *Irresistible Faith*.[1] Among other things, he brilliantly illuminated the reality that the world will be irresistibly drawn not to those who appear artificially flawless, but to those who are transparent about the fact that their human frailty and weakness is sustained only by an outside force that now dwells in them. Scott stated—correctly, in my view—that his congregation and others benefit more from Christ followers who know they walk with a limp than those who pretend they have it all together.

To put it plainly, many of us are dead because we are hesitant to ask for true life to fill us. We walk with a limp, but our efforts are channeled toward masking the limp rather than accepting an infilling that will conquer that limp and lend a magnetism to our walk that draws others in ways we cannot imagine.

We are presently dead. But the sovereign Lord is asking us if we can live. He wants to know if we believe it. If we do, He will ask us to speak life into the dead bones around us. He will provide the breath and cover the bones with flesh, but He is asking us to speak out and call that life forth. He wants us to proclaim that life. He wants us to be participants in the calling forth of His church.

This is where it gets exciting. For too long I have read Ezekiel 37 as simply a powerful promise that life is available to us. I have read it as a story of life conquering death, and of restoration and resurrection of that which is lost. I have read it as a promise that any of us, no matter how depraved, can be brought to a place of realizing God's great power. All those things are certainly true.

But for those who follow Jesus, it is so much more than that!

Notice what Ezekiel called the collection of bones that came to life. He did not number them or address them as individuals. Rather, he said, "So I prophesied as he commanded me, and breath entered them; they came to life and stood up on their feet—*a vast army.*"

A vast army! I believe those three words change the game for those of us who would dare make this request. We are not called to rise as individuals. Yes, we each have an individual choice to make, but in reality we are a vast army that is too often just a valley of dry, dead bones. We must each choose to request His fame, and He is desperate to know us personally and intimately, but this call to elevate His fame is one that is done together. It is one that requires being shoulder to shoulder with our fellow believers.

This request for more of God's power and fame is not one that can be done alone. It will require a vast army fully dedicated to the Famous One. As each of us rises individually, we add to the ranks of a church that is rising and standing as one, and we begin to form a force for His fame against which no evil can stand.

It is a team sport. We will do this together, or we will not do it at all. What is holding us back? What is keeping us dry and dead? Where are we being called to serve? What has prevented us from joining the vast army that is coming to life? Too often, I fear it has been a hesitancy to unify with our brothers and sisters of the faith.

No more! Our hesitancy to join the ranks has left a hole in the line. It has left us vulnerable, and it has left the church vulnerable. Yes, there will be instances of iron sharpening iron and of internal and honest grappling over disagreements, but that must be done within the context of a unified and cohesive unit. That must be done after acknowledging there is a hole in the ranks of this vast army that you and I are meant to fill.

It is time for the bones to come together.

It is time for tendons and flesh and skin to cover the bones.

And it is time for the breath of the sovereign Lord to move through the dead lungs.

It is time for our now-living bodies to stand up on our feet.

It is time for us to form a vast army. An army with a mission to proclaim the Famous One.

No more are we divided, and no more are our requests many. We have but one request, and it pertains to His fame and His mighty deeds: "Repeat them again in our day, in our time make them known; in wrath remember mercy."

Do it again, God!

CHAPTER 14

IN THE HANDS OF
A MIGHTY GOD

*For the kingdom of God is not a
matter of talk but of power.*

—1 CORINTHIANS 4:20

I steer clear of things that can kill me."

I was working to remove an old and broken gaslight from our property. Brooke, knowing my preference for learning how to complete tasks myself (not to mention my reputation for being on the cheap side), asked what made me decide to call in a professional to help with the capping of the gas line. I responded, "I steer clear of things that can kill me."

It sounds overly dramatic, but it really is a guiding principle for me when I take on projects (which I love to do). There is very little that makes me as happy as a weekend or some time off with the calendar clear to tackle a project around the house. I love to build furniture, repair structures, install equipment—you name it. I enjoy the actual work, yes, but a huge part of my enjoyment comes from the task of figuring out how to do something new. In the age of YouTube and Google, I hold a firm belief that nearly everyone can complete almost any household task if they just possess a little curiosity. If you combine the most basic handyman skills with an insatiable curiosity, a willingness to make a mistake or two along the way, and twenty-first-century information sharing, you can accomplish almost any home project.

To embrace this mind-set, however, it is critical to understand when it is acceptable to make mistakes and when a mistake could be catastrophic. It is important to know your limitations and to recognize when the consequences of exceeding those limitations could cause real harm. If you are painting a piece of furniture and are unsure whether you have the skill required, I recommend you muster the courage to study the technique options and then give it a try. The worst you can do is not really harmful, and the best you can do is surprise yourself with a beautiful result. But if you need a gas line or a circuit breaker installed, and you are not sufficiently experienced with how the power behind these items operates, you need a professional or you might end up dead!

So if I am dealing with gas or electrical that requires expertise beyond a fairly elementary level, I call in the pros, usually my neighbor Chris. This approach actually allows me to accomplish far more than I otherwise could, because as long as I know I am taking on tasks that will not kill or harm me, I am free to give it my best shot and see what happens. After all, what is the worst that could go wrong as long as I steer clear of the things that can kill me?

This approach works great for projects around the house. But, my friends, for too long we have used it as a reason to steer clear of the power that is offered to us if we will submit to being used by the mighty hands of God. We know that His power is infinitely mighty, and certainly possesses the power to destroy, so we follow our handyman advice and avoid that which could kill us. But it is a mistake with consequences beyond just physical harm or death. It is a mistake of voluntarily laying down the very purpose for which we were created—the prospect of being used by our Creator.

Is He powerful to the point of being dangerous? Yes, He is. But the danger is not one that should deter us from drawing near; no, the real danger is to the forces of injustice and evil. It is a danger we are called to step into without hesitancy or fear. It is one that calls us away from playing it safe and into being used in accordance with His power. Ironically, there is nothing safe about playing it safe, and nowhere are we more secure than in the midst of His power.

For far too much of my life, I have lived safely. I have made decisions based primarily on avoiding the things that can kill me. That mentality comes at a cost. It keeps us from engaging the things that matter most, and prevents us from leading lives to the fullness of His design. We were created to be instruments in His hand, and to reach a world of people with His message of love and power. But to be an instrument in the mighty hand of God, we have to be willing to be held in and by His power.

"It is a dreadful thing to fall into the hands of the living

God" (Heb. 10:31). It strikes me there are two sides to that coin. First, it is clearly dreadful to meet God's vengeance when it comes against sin. But conversely, it is an indescribably awesome proposition to consider falling into His hands for the purpose of being used by Him. Candidly, it is the only life goal truly worth pursuing.

Could it kill me? Yes, it could. Do I desperately want to place myself in His hands anyway? More than anything.

MORE THAN JUDGMENT

In 1741, Jonathan Edwards famously preached about "sinners in the hands of an angry God." His message was a sober (and true) proclamation about our desperate need for grace to save us from our deserved damnation. Edwards spoke of the reality of a God whose patience will eventually run out, and he exhorted believers to repent before it is too late. It was a powerful sermon, and one that remains rooted in the psyche of many believers today. The sermon was effective because it so vividly illustrated the judgment side of God's character and fame. It is a message that is still true and relevant for us today.

But while many of us continue to accept the truth of Edwards's famous sermon, I think we have largely forgotten the other side of the coin. We have forgotten that God's infinite power was not created only for wrath. Quite the contrary, it was created to work through us for the purpose of reaching a world in need. We were created to be instruments that deliver the vast power of a mighty God. Our experience with God is tragically short-circuited if it culminates only in the receipt of His judgment-averting grace.

No, His plan for us is that we would use the receipt of His grace as a foundation from which to go into all the world and spread His fame. He wants to show off His power and fame, and He wants to do it through us. That is why He sent us His grace and afforded us the possibility of averting His judgment.

The prospect of being a sinner in the hands of an angry God is not a pleasant one. But let us not make the mistake of viewing that image as part of God's plan for us, or wrongly conclude we are not designed to be used by His hands. God's blueprint is that we would be instruments in the hands of a mighty God! His desire is that we would be an extension of Himself with the capability of changing the world.

So it is time to lay aside the paralyzing portion of the trepidation that comes with considering God's wrath. Rather, it is time to live boldly expectant of a move of God, and equally expectant that the move will occur through us. We are not to be satisfied to simply avert the destructive wrath of an angry God. We are to insist upon our birthright that affords us access to the life-giving and saving power of the cross!

Will there sometimes still be trepidation as we take on His power? Yes! That is to be expected. But it is nothing compared to the trepidation we should feel at the prospect of forfeiting the opportunity to be used by His hand.

SPARED FOR A PURPOSE

God wanted to kill Moses. We accurately think of Moses as a hero of faith, and in doing so we conveniently set aside certain parts of his story, including the fact that God's anger burned against

Moses to the point of deciding to end his life. God had planned to use Moses but was now fed up and ready to kill him.

The story is found in Exodus 4 as God is calling Moses to return to Egypt and lead the Israelites out of captivity. As we are so prone to respond, Moses is focused more on his lack of ability than on the magnitude of God's ability, and he continues to resist.

"What if they do not believe me or listen to me?" (v. 1)

"I have never been eloquent" (v. 10).

"I am slow of speech and tongue" (v. 10).

"Please send someone else" (v. 13).

Moses has seen God perform wonder after wonder, and yet he still falls into the trap of believing that the task to which he has been called must be accomplished in his own human strength. He has just witnessed God perform tangible, in-the-flesh miracles, and yet when that same God assigns him a task along with a promise to go with him, Moses feels the need to inventory his skills and weigh them against the size of the task. He still thinks it depends on him.

Finally, God's anger starts to reach a boiling point, but He relents and agrees to send the well-spoken and polished Aaron to share in the assignment (vv. 14–17). It is God's way of relenting to Moses. But His anger did not subside.

As Moses begins his journey to Egypt, he stops for the night to rest. Apparently, God's anger had continued to simmer, because verse 24 says that God "met Moses and was about to kill him." God's impatience with Moses's disbelief was so great that He again decided to kill Moses and choose another to take his place. It was only because of the dramatic intervention of Moses' wife Zipporah that Moses was spared (vv. 25–26).

But why? Why, if God was so fed up with Moses' stubbornness and doubt, did He decide to spare his life? Surely God could have accomplished His plan to rescue the Israelites through someone else. Surely Moses, like all of us, was replaceable in that sense. Surely the Creator of the universe would not have been left without options if Moses were out of the equation. So what caused God to stay His hand?

It was not that Moses was indispensable.

It was not that God was out of options.

It was that God *desired* Moses.

It was that God did not simply desire for His fame to be known but rather longed to make His fame known *through Moses*.

Yes, God's primary aim was, and always is, His own fame. But hopefully by this point, none of us are surprised that God's design for lifting high His name and fame runs through us! He does not desire a fame that is separate from relationship with us, but rather He desires a fame that is made great as a result of a relationship with us. He longs for His name to be praised through the work in which He has assigned us a partnership. He longs for His purposes to be entangled and intertwined within His relationship with us.

God's desire to show off His power through relationship with Moses was strong enough to overcome His wrath toward Moses. It was also strong enough to stay His hand against a stubborn pharaoh for a time. God instructed Moses to deliver this message to Pharaoh,

> Let my people go, so that they may worship me, or this time I
> will send the full force of my plagues against you and against
> your officials and your people, so you may know that there is no

one like me in all the earth. For by now I could have stretched out my hand and struck you and your people with a plague that would have wiped you off the earth. But I have raised you up for this very purpose, that I might show you my power and that my name might be proclaimed in all the earth. (Ex. 9:13–16)

"I have raised you up [some translations say, 'I have spared you'] for this very purpose, that I might show you my power and that my name might be proclaimed in all the earth."

God spared Pharaoh (for a time) so that His own power and name might be proclaimed throughout the land.

God spared Moses as a means of fully displaying His own fame.

God has shown patience with me so that I might make His fame known.

God has raised you up and is calling you to His purposes not that you might be famous. No, His purpose in calling you is so much greater. He has raised you up, He has called you to His side, and He has spared you for one reason—that His power and fame might be proclaimed through your life in all the land.

You were created to live in and be used by the hands of a mighty God.

IF NOT YOU, THEN WHO?

We have all had the same doubts and the same questions about our qualifications and abilities as did Moses. Think through the excuses that Moses had and consider how many of them have applied to your life.

First, Moses doubted his human abilities. "I have never been eloquent . . . I am slow of speech and tongue." This occurs to me on a daily basis. I fear I am not smart enough, or educated enough, or connected enough, or whatever-it-is enough to carry out God's call. I have no doubt you can relate, because it is a human condition to weigh our qualifications against the task at hand. But we have to remember, God has called us to tasks that are bigger than us in order to reveal *His* glory, not ours! We have missed the main point. If we only complete tasks for which we are equipped, we will be tempted to take credit. Even if we try to give God the glory, the world will default to a belief that we did it on our own merit. There is nothing particularly breathtaking about the completion of tasks within our abilities and qualifications. So God has called us beyond those so that He might get the glory.

Next, Moses asks, "What if they do not believe me or listen to me?" We all ask some version of this question. What if it fails? What if no one pays any attention? What if I look foolish? My friends, obedience is ours, but results are His. On the one hand, we will not always have assurance that the things we set our hands to will succeed. In fact, the primary purpose of His instruction is often simply our obedience rather than the ensuing outcome. But it is also true that we dramatically underestimate the power of our God to do things "immeasurably more than all we ask or imagine" (Eph. 3:20). Scripture is replete with similar promises, but I think my favorite is Psalm 37:5: "Commit your way to the LORD; trust in him and he will do this."

He will do it. In fact, He will do it again—just as He did in days past. But we must commit it to Him. Obedience is ours; outcomes are His.

Finally, in a foreshadowing of what may be the most common

of our refusals, Moses begs, "Please send someone else." We always think God could pick someone better. Even Moses—the great hero of faith—fell for this lie. It seems ridiculous to us, because we know the final legacy of Moses. But in his own mind, Moses felt every bit the stammering, stuttering murderer that he was. Surely God could find someone better! Why had God chosen him? If only Moses had been able to view his life from God's perspective, he would have been able to see the unique imprint on his life—an imprint made by the very fingerprints of God. Yes, he was fatally flawed. We all are. But this was the task for which he had been created. There was no one else to send. God had not made a mistake.

God has not made a mistake with you, either. I am convinced that if you knew the end of your story, it would seem equally ridiculous for you to ask these doubting questions of God. If you could see the view God has of you, it would be unthinkable to question the fact that God has called you.

You feel unqualified. And it is true. We are all, in fact, unqualified. But your God can do all things through you (Phil. 4:13).

You are afraid it will fail. It may. But why is that possibility so paralyzing? Because results are up to God, and your God might do exceedingly abundantly more than you can ask or imagine. Is not that possibility worth the risk of failure? Obedience is yours; outcomes are His.

Finally, you would prefer He send someone else. I have news for you: there is no one else. Only you. You were uniquely created for the tasks to which He is calling you. There is only you because He deeply desires you. If you do not respond, then who will? If you do not fill the place in the ranks He has prepared for you, then who will? If not you, then who?

I will say it again. There is no one else. Only you.

CHAPTER 15

. . . .

MERCY ADVOCATES

*Speak and act as those who are going to
be judged by the law that gives freedom,
because judgment without mercy will
be shown to anyone who has not been
merciful. Mercy triumphs over judgment.*

—JAMES 2:12–13

Washington, DC, has been our family's home for almost twenty years now. During that time, we have grown from two single individuals into a family of five, plus a dog and a turtle! We have come to love and embrace "our city" and the wonderful opportunities it affords us. At the same time, Brooke will always be an Idaho girl at heart, and I will always call the cornfields of central Illinois home. We generally make at least one trip per year back to each "home" to visit family and take a break.

Recently, we have added a tradition to our annual Illinois trip. Because we typically fly in and out of Chicago before driving downstate, we have started to schedule a day or two in the Windy City before heading home. Chicago has always been the large city I most associate with, and Brooke and the kids really enjoy it as well. We catch a Cubs game, visit a local attraction, eat some deep-dish pizza, and just generally take in the sights. It is a great way to finish off a family trip, and all the walking typically burns off any extra energy the kids have. (Brooke and I do not have extra energy.)

Because of all the walking, we do our best to pack light. I have always been a minimalist when it comes to packing or carrying stuff with me, and we are learning as a family to get along with less when we travel or go camping. Even so, on this particular Chicago day, we somehow managed to fill an entire backpack with snacks, water, coats, and so forth. I was not sure how or why it was so full and so heavy, but I toted that thing around the city all day, because that is what a good dad is supposed to do! We had a great time—Navy Pier, Shedd's Aquarium, Lake Michigan, and a boat ride on the Chicago River.

As we returned to the hotel that evening, we were all pretty spent. As everyone took their coats and shoes off, I slipped the backpack off with a bit of relief and wondered again why it was so heavy. I figured I was just getting old or had been skipping too many workouts. But while both of those things may have been part of the problem, I was about to discover another major contributing factor.

After taking out all the coats and snacks and water bottles,

I discovered that someone had put two rather large chunks of concrete into the bottom of the backpack! Unbeknown to me, I had been carrying those two pieces of concrete on my back for the entire day. When I asked the kids why in the world there was concrete in the backpack, Hope earnestly replied, "Well, they are my special rocks, and I didn't want to leave them at the hotel!"

DON'T CARRY YOUR ROCKS

In many ways, the memory of carrying Hope's concrete "rocks" is endearing and humorous. I love her affinity for things everyone else overlooks or even discards. I hope she never loses that trait. But at the same time, there is simply no way in the world those concrete chunks would have been allowed to go into my backpack had I known about them. In fact, there is no way they would have made it into Hope's travel bag from home had they been discovered. I also have to wonder what the TSA agents thought when they saw two chunks of concrete in the luggage. It is a wonder we escaped extra screening.

It is also similar to how we treat this wonderful gift called mercy.

First and foremost, we—undeserving sinners—all have the weight of sin in our life. Romans 3:23 says, "for all have sinned and fall short of the glory of God." The penalty for that sin is the heavy weight of eternal death (Rom. 6:23). All of us are responsible for and deserve the weight of the rocks we have put into our bags and are carrying around on our backs. Like Hope's special rocks, they are heavy and burdensome. Unlike Hope's rocks, they lead to eternal separation from God if we insist on continuing to carry them.

The great news of the gospel is that we do not have to carry any rocks beyond those we refuse to take out of our bags. Yes, we are all responsible for our own burdens of sin, but the terrific grant of mercy afforded us at the cross means we no longer have to carry that burden! The sacrifice made at the cross means we do not have to be weighed down by our sin. We can be free of it.

The wages of sin is death, but the remainder of that verse says, "but the gift of God is eternal life through Christ Jesus our Lord." The penalty has already been paid, and we are invited to be free of it forever.

So why do we insist on refusing that gift in its entirety? Why do we believe that our sin requires walking around forever with the shame and the guilt associated with that sin? If we have been offered a free pardon and a complete unburdening of that sin, why do so many of us continue to pick up the burden of our guilt when we do not have to? Why do we insist on assuming the identity of guilt when we have been granted a full pardon?

My friends, I am keenly aware that the weight of sin is heavy. It exists in my own life, and there are moments when its weight slows me down. We are all sinners. But we can be free of the weight associated with that sin. We have been granted mercy upon mercy, and our ability to be a force for the kingdom will be infinitely greater if we choose to embrace that mercy.

Take the rocks out of your backpack. The price for them has already been paid in full at the cross. It is the very reason that Jesus endured the cross. Will we really smite His sacrifice by insisting the price He paid was not high enough? No more! Leave the rocks behind—they are no longer yours to carry.

DO NOT LET OTHERS CARRY YOUR ROCKS

As hard as it can be to walk in freedom from our sin, it may be even more difficult to grant mercy to those who have wronged us. It really should not be difficult considering the mercy that has been shown to us, but I know how often I have instead chosen to hold a grudge. Even though I have been allowed to lay down my burden of sin, I tend to be hesitant to allow others to unload their burdens if they involve a wrong committed against me. In a very real sense, they are carrying around my concrete rocks, and I am insisting they not lay them down.

The danger here is real. It is certainly true that God's grant of mercy is abounding. It is plentiful and freely available to each of us. His mercy is what overwhelms the judgment we deserve at His hand. But we must take heed that it will not be granted to those who do not themselves offer mercy.

James 2:13 says, "because judgment without mercy will be shown to anyone who has not been merciful." Habakkuk was afraid to embrace the fame of God partly because he knew about the wrath of God. So when Habakkuk finally stepped forward, and when he received an answer that contained a significant dose of coming judgment, he pleaded, "In wrath remember mercy."

Mercy overwhelms judgment. Mercy triumphs over judgment. We have been shown mercy over mercy and can be free of judgment. But if we do not show mercy, we will be judged without mercy. God help us!

Do not let others carry around rocks on your behalf. Do not let them shoulder burdens that you can unload by granting forgiveness. It is quite possible—probable, even—they do not deserve your mercy. That is really the point. They do not deserve it, but neither do you. Neither do I. We do not deserve mercy, and yet we have been granted it. All that is required of us is that we in turn grant undeserved mercy.

Do not let others carry your rocks.

BE A MERCY ADVOCATE

To fully immerse ourselves in this amazing thing called grace, we have talked about the importance of allowing the weight of our sin to be fully lifted from us. We have also explored the reality that to be afforded mercy and forgiveness, we must be merciful to those who have wronged us. There is a symbiotic relationship between our receipt of mercy and our willingness to grant mercy. It requires both sides of the equation to genuinely possess either one. If we resist mercy for our wrongs, we will not have the capacity to grant mercy. If we refuse to grant mercy, we will not be afforded mercy from above.

Now I want to challenge us to embrace a mercy that goes beyond ourselves. In a way, the two-sided mercy we have covered so far is primarily for ourselves. Yes, granting mercy can lift burdens from others and show the love of God. But it is also simply a requirement we must fulfill if we want to receive His mercy. Now, as we pursue what it looks like to live for a purpose beyond ourselves, I want to spur us on to a third element of mercy that transcends what is beneficial to or required of us. To fully dwell in this concept of mercy, I believe we must become mercy advocates for others.

When Jesus, hanging from the cross, said, "Father, forgive them, for they do not know what they are doing" (Luke 23:34), He was granting mercy to those who had wronged Him. But when He stood between a woman accused of adultery and a mob of religious zealots who wanted to stone her, and said, "Let any one of you who is without sin be the first to throw a stone at her," He was advocating for mercy to be shown to someone who had not wronged Him (John 8:7). He was engaging on the side of mercy on behalf of someone who was outside of the James 2:13 requirement to show mercy as we have been shown mercy.

Instead, Jesus was walking in Habakkuk 3:2 mercy: "In wrath remember mercy." He was taking up the cause for someone whose guilt did not involve Him. He was choosing to advocate for mercy in a way that expanded the reach of God's fame.

This gentle act of mercy becomes even more powerful when we realize the woman's guilt was likely fairly apparent. The story describes Jesus stooping to write in the dirt before answering. While John's account does not specifically confirm this, Jesus was in all likelihood fulfilling the requirement of the law that the name of the accused and the crime committed be written down.[1] He was demonstrating that the mercy He was about to call for was not motivated by a belief the woman was innocent. In fact, He likely knew she was guilty. But He was taking a stand for mercy, anyway.

As the woman's accusers began to leave, Jesus asked her, "Woman, where are they? Has no one condemned you?"

"No one, sir," she said.

"Then neither do I condemn you," Jesus declared. "Go now and leave your life of sin." (John 8:9–11)

Jesus knew of her guilt, and her wrongs had not been committed against Him. But He stepped between the accusers and the accused anyway and advocated for mercy. He did not advocate for a statement of innocence but for a grant of mercy. Once mercy had been attained, He called the woman to leave her life of sin.

How often do we emulate this model of mercy? How often do we find far more comfort in a rush to embrace justice that satisfies our bloodthirst for every wrong to be rectified? How eager are we to be advocates for mercy in situations that do not directly involve us?

Please hear me: I am most decidedly not advocating against consequences for sin or crime. Appropriate consequences are necessary for both repentance and deterrence and have an absolutely essential role in society. But that essential role does not justify the bloodthirst for punishment that too often exists in my heart. It does not change my call to be on the lookout for those to whom mercy might be appropriately granted. It does not negate my duty to engage when my voice might possibly be the difference between indiscriminate and unproductive judgment and a grant of mercy that results in the restoration and reconciliation of the guilty.

Must the innocent be protected and defended? Absolutely! They—the widow and the orphan, especially—are our first charge. When the guilty continue to pose a threat to the innocent, the judgment they have earned must not be lifted.

But when we are advocating for judgment as a means to simply satiate our thirst for vengeance, we are not following in the footsteps of Jesus of Nazareth.

Wrath and mercy work together to proclaim the fame of God. Without mercy, God's wrath would be destructive and boundless—which is why He has tempered it with mercy. His mercy without judgment would be permissive to the point of enabling wrongdoing—which is why His mercy is offered only to those who would themselves show mercy.

We have been given mercy.

We must grant mercy.

And we must advocate for mercy.

WE CAN BE THE FATHER

There is no doubt that God's fame has tremendous power. It is absolutely holy and therefore contains sobering justice and judgment. But the hallmark of God's fame is an ever-present and always-abundant grant of mercy and grace. His love for us abounds to an extent that He desires none would perish (2 Peter 3:9), and His patience for our obedience is constantly on display. The justice side of this equation tends to attract the spotlight, but the real glory of God's fame is found in His mercy. Habakkuk seemed initially hesitant, and maybe even a tad fearful, and his plea for God's fame to again roll through the land closed appropriately with a reminder that our human frailty needs the fame of God to be tempered with His mercy: "In wrath remember mercy."

The concept of undeserved mercy is beautifully illustrated in the parable of the prodigal son. It is a familiar story to many of us of a son who squanders his inheritance and is forced to return to his father with hat in hand, begging to simply become a servant in his father's household in order to survive. The father has every right to respond punitively. After all, his son has deeply wronged him, and has destroyed much of the fruit from his life's work. But instead, the father instantly forgives and forgets the wrong committed against him. He eagerly embraces his son and calls for a celebration because the son has come home. It is not only mercy where wrath was due; it is a celebration and a path toward full restoration.

I find it easy to relate to the son. As I have grown closer to God, I have grappled with a deeper realization of my own depravity. The extent of my realization that I am undeserving of His mercy has grown, and it has been necessary to remind myself that the magnitude of my sin is not cause for defeat, but rather a reminder of just how great a gift I have been given.

My guess is that you also can relate to the son. But did you realize that while we have received mercy as the son did, the story is also a call for us to be the father? We are called to receive with open arms those who have earned our wrath and retribution and to provide them instead with forgiveness, restoration, and celebration. This is one of the most effective tools for facilitating the spread of God's fame.

I love how the story says, "But while he was still a long way off, his father saw him and was filled with compassion for him; he ran to his son, threw his arms around him and kissed him" (Luke 15:20). I think instantly of my son, Jude. I think of my daughters, Brell and Hope. I know this is how I would feel if they were in need of mercy. But it is not so easy when others commit the wrongs.

"But while he was still a long way off, his father saw him and was filled with compassion for him." The father had been actively looking for his son and eagerly anticipating his return. He was not surprised and forced to make a spur-of-the-moment decision about forgiveness. Rather, he was actively watching and waiting for him. He noticed him well before he arrived and ran to him to ensure he knew he was welcomed home.

Are we considering forgiveness only when those who have wronged us come back to us? Or are we going beyond? If we want to be like the father, we must be actively seeking out those who have wronged us—or otherwise gone astray—so that we might see them while they are still a long way off. I know it sounds crazy, but that is when we must run to them. That is where the real opportunity for restoration lies, because it is the run to those who are in the wrong that communicates they are truly welcomed home. It is our eagerness to be with them that says they are celebrated.

We identify with the prodigal son, but we are called to be the father.

We deserve wrath. But we have been given abundant mercy. As we step forward to carry the fame of God into our world, and as we expectantly call for it to show up in mighty ways we could not even imagine, we must constantly wrap that fame in a message full of God's mercy.

It is mercy that makes His justice complete.

It is mercy that makes His judgment just.

And it is mercy that ignites the spread of His fame.

Therefore, a depiction of God's fame is not accurate if it is not cloaked in His mercy. We must be more than simply recipients of His mercy. We must become advocates for it.

CHAPTER 16

. . . .

THE END OF OUR STORIES

It is done. I am the Alpha and the Omega,
the Beginning and the End. To the thirsty
I will give water without cost from the
spring of the water of life. Those who are
victorious will inherit all this, and I will be
their God and they will be my children.
—REVELATION 21:6–7

I can't leave the last pages empty. I have to decide how I want
my story to end."

Our then-nine-year-old son, Jude, had undertaken the task
of writing a book, and his statement about how he was thinking
about the last chapter stopped me in my tracks. In my view, his

story was complete, even though some of the pages of his make-shift book were empty. But he saw the empty pages as needing to be filled. He saw them not as extra pages that could simply be removed, but as a blank slate that gave him an opportunity to select a closing narrative of his choosing.

It is a remarkable parallel to the way all of us think, really, because each of us is looking for a way to fill the pages of our life, and especially looking for a way to finish our story. We are seeking a closing narrative that will leave behind a legacy of greatness. We are hoping to close out our life in a way that is worth something to those we leave behind. Granted, maybe the best way to leave behind something of worth is to focus more intensely on preparing for the beautiful reunion with our Creator that is to come. Even so, if we have learned anything in these pages, we should be convinced that our time and work here on earth matter, and we should commit to use both for the maximum glory of His name.

It is exciting to consider that we get to play such a large role in the writing of our own stories. We get to select our own narratives and even some of the closing chapter—though the conclusion has already been written. Even more exhilarating, we have been invited to hide our stories inside the greatest story ever told. We have been given permission to make our stories a part of His story, and to apply the influence of our lives toward His fame. We do not have to dream up, or work to create, a compelling narrative that will leave a legacy. Instead, we are eagerly invited to enter into a narrative that is beyond anything we could have believed even if we had been told. Does that promise sound familiar? It is not speculation. He has promised He is going to do it. The question is whether or not we will decide to take part in it.

So how do we select a closing narrative and an end to our earthly stories that reflects His fame?

THE MIDDLE CHAPTERS

"It is finished" (John 19:30).

Jesus mustered up the last of His physical strength and the last of His dying breath to utter those words. In doing so, He announced the end of the fully human portion of His story. He proclaimed that His pre-resurrection work had been accomplished. He articulated that He had given His all. From a human perspective, it is a feeling I long to have when my time comes. I want to be able to look back from my deathbed with satisfaction not on what I have accomplished but on what the Father has been able to do through me. I want a closing chapter that is marked with assurance that my work on earth is complete. I want to leave a legacy of a life spent and given for the Name above every other name. I want to be able to look back with satisfaction as a result of my life's work being complete rather than celebrated. I long for my story to be woven into His and for my fame to be hidden in His. Oh, to be able to say, "It is finished."

But these final words of Jesus from the cross declared much more than just the end of His earthly story. They also declared the end of our earthly stories. They serve as an eternal reminder that we need not fear how to fill the rest of our lives' pages, because He has already written them. In fact, He has already performed them. The pressure is off.

In so many ways, I long for finality. Or maybe it is more accurate to say I long for the assurance of finality. I want to know what the end looks like. But the truth is, I already have that assurance. One of the greatest beauties of the cross is that the sacrifice made upon it wrote the end of my story. It wrote the end of yours as well. We not only know the end, but we know that we win in the end!

This concept is far more than just a promise that makes us feel good. Instead, if we take hold of it, it should fill us with immense freedom for how we choose to fill the pages of our lives between now and our deaths. If ends of our stories have been written, the only question remaining is, How will we write the chapters leading up to the conclusion?

As we consider the beautiful reality that He is the Alpha and the Omega, the Beginning and the End, I think we will find there is only one truly worthwhile use of those beautiful middle chapters He has entrusted to us. There is only one way for those remaining portions to fit into the larger story, and it is by aiming them in the direction of His glory. The story becomes not only finished but also complete when we dedicate the middle chapters to the purpose of His fame.

Ecclesiastes 3 gives us a beautiful picture of this concept. It begins with the familiar refrain, "There is a time for everything, and a season for every activity under the heavens: a time to be born and a time to die, . . . a time to weep and a time to laugh, a time to mourn and a time to dance" (Eccl. 3:1–2, 4). Already, the passage is speaking to this idea of how we should spend our lives. But then comes this transitional declaration:

> He has made everything beautiful in its time. He has also set
> eternity in the human heart; yet no one can fathom what God
> has done from beginning to end. I know that there is nothing

better for people than to be happy and to do good while they live. That each of them may eat and drink, and find satisfaction in all their toil—this is the gift of God. (Eccl. 3:11–13)

My friends, it is true we cannot see God's entire plan. It is true we will be bewildered about why some of His plan unfolds the way it does. But it is just as true that He has both set a desire for eternity in our hearts and called us to a specific work for His glory on this earth. It is why He has sent His power for our use and invited us to walk in it—because our task is really His task. Our mission is His mission, and it will require His power.

Here is the reality: I am useless for the kingdom but for Him working through me. You are worthless for the kingdom but for Him working through you.

But I am what moves His power into action. You are what moves His power into action. If we do not move, His power stays on the sideline. Our participation is integral and essential if His kingdom is to be realized here on earth in our time. We are worthless for the kingdom but for His power, but we are irreplaceable as vessels by which His power and fame are carried to the needs of our world.

He has chosen to stay His hand until we step forward. He has done so because He deeply desires a relationship with us. It is time to use our middle chapters to step forward and watch Him do things beyond our wildest imaginations. Even that is not really a high enough aim. No, it is time to step forward and participate in things beyond our wildest imaginations. It is time to step forward and be the *catalyst for* things beyond our wildest imaginations.

It is time to live only for His fame.

HEADING HOME

This world is not our home. Philippians 3:20 says that our "citizenship is in heaven," and Hebrews 13:14 says, "we do not have an enduring city, but we are looking for the city that is to come." In other words, we are just passing through this temporary home and are on our way to the home that has been prepared for us.

A firm grasp of this reality can help us draw near to Jesus while relaxing our hold on things of this world. When all is said and done, nothing this world has to offer can compare with—or even add to—being found in Him. When we walk in understanding that we are not home yet, it becomes natural to leave aside the pursuits of this world in exchange for simply knowing, walking with, and serving Jesus. Without Him, we have nothing. With Him, we lack nothing.

Proximity to our Savior should take priority over every other pursuit. But the power of this concept is lost if our focus on eternity causes us to miss the very reason we are journeying through our current world. We certainly do not want to be attached to this world, but we cannot be so oblivious that we forget we have been called to it.

This world is not where we belong, but it is absolutely where we have been sent!

It is not an accident we are here. It is not a glitch in God's plan. In fact, it is a primary feature of God's plan. He could have just gathered us to Himself, but instead He sent us to a temporary place—one with very real struggles and challenges—that we might invite others to join us in our eternal home.

Because of this call to work in one world while committing our hearts to another, we will always need to struggle against competing devotions. We may commit to living for His glory, but we must continually ask ourselves, *Do I mean it? When all is stripped away, will I be at peace?* When my platform crumbles, or my project fails, or my influence is tarnished or diminished, will my spirit still be at rest as a result of my heart being devoted to my eternal home?

In my own experience, it is a struggle that is never fully overcome, but it is one so very worth engaging. If we want to look back on lives that were spent for His glory, we must shift our everyday focus away from self-preservation and toward those around us. We must strive to hold others up. We must prefer their name to ours and His name above all names.

When we acknowledge that this world is not our home, it should remind us that the struggles of this life are but temporary.

When we properly desire only a pursuit of and a proximity to our Savior, it should free us from attachments to this world because nothing can be added to the joy of being found in Him.

When we remember that our citizenship is in heaven, it should both assure us that we already belong to Him and motivate us to use the time He has given us on earth for His glory.

We are not home yet, but we are heading home. In the meantime, there is work for us to do in this place.

UNITY IN THE GATHERING

Our coming reunion with Jesus is often referred to as a marriage banquet. Matthew 22 and Revelation 21 are two prominent examples. I have often wondered what it will feel like to enter into that banquet. What an incomprehensible moment it will be to slip the temporal bonds of flesh and together with fellow believers enter into eternity as wedding bells toll for us!

As I imagine that day, I find myself mainly focused on two things: the anticipation and the gathering.

First, the anticipation. I think of the 2017 Major League Baseball playoffs when my Chicago Cubs faced the Washington Nationals for a five-game series. Naturally, given that games one, two, and five were played in our local Washington, DC, area, Jude and I wanted to attend. But tickets were in high demand and expensive, so we ended up with two standing-room tickets for the first couple of games. That required us to arrive early and claim a place next to the outfield gate so that we might be the first ones to rush inside and stake a spot with an unobstructed view for Jude.

As we waited outside the gate each night and as people started to crowd in around us, the buzz of anticipation built to a palpable level. The idea of waiting to be let into a highly anticipated event was exhilarating. Of course that was but a microscopic taste of what it will be like to gather for the purpose of entering into our own heavenly wedding banquet!

Second, and probably more significant, I am so eager for the gathering of all God's people together as one. I can hardly imagine the feeling of gathering with fellow believers from across history with wedding bells ringing. After generations of division, what an amazing show of unity it will be to stand together in that eternal place!

My friend and pastor Joshua Symonette said, "God's fame is revealed through the unity of His creation." That is what I imagine this heavenly moment will feel like. Yes, we are called to carry the fame of God into this earthly realm, but the full essence of His fame will be felt and on display as people from

every tongue, tribe, and time gather together for one purpose—
the celebration of our unity with Him!

My friends, we see so dimly now. But we will see fully then. I
will have been wrong about something. You will have been wrong
about something. The question when we gather in eternity will
not be about which of us was correct on which issues, but rather
how we will be found to have treated our brothers and sisters in
Christ who disagreed with us. Was it cause for division on earth?
Or did it spur us to extend our mercy to others? In that moment,
the only thing that will matter is our unity in Jesus. May we find
just a bit more of that unity on this side of eternity.

DEDICATED TO FAME

I imagine many of you are wondering how the story of Habakkuk—
the prophet who confronted God—ends. We already know that
God did not rush to grant Habakkuk's request immediately and
exactly as Habakkuk envisioned. But more important, how did
a God with the power to create and destroy all that we know
respond to one of His small created beings who had the audacity
to decry His absence? What did the God of the universe say to the
one who dared to confront Him in a time of need?

We find the answer in the very last verse of Habakkuk.
Habakkuk's story ends with a prayer that is really a proclamation
of God's fame. It is a triumphal celebration of God's power that
opens with the now-familiar cry for God's fame to be repeated in
the present day. But it closes with this stirring declaration: "The
Sovereign LORD is my strength; he makes my feet like the feet of
a deer, he enables me to tread on the heights" (Hab. 3:19).

Habakkuk's obedience began with a recitation of God's fame. The recitation was followed by a call for God's fame to reemerge through Habakkuk in a redemptive way. It ends with Habakkuk's claim of God's promise to set him upon high places and provide sound footing. It is a promise of old that remains alive today as we face perilous times. It is a promise offered freely to us. He will carry us to high places, and He will set us upon solid ground. It is a promise that is set into motion when we dedicate ourselves to His fame.

As we think about how we want the earthly portion of our stories to end, let us choose narratives that prevent it from ending at all. Let us dedicate ourselves fully to the task of amplifying the name of the Famous One and to calling others into an eternity with Him. Let us fill those remaining pages of our lives not with stories of our fame, but rather with proclamations of His fame. Greater still, let us learn to invite His power and fame to routinely fill us and be poured out of us for the benefit of the world around us. Let us choose to use all our days from this one to our last for the purpose of His fame.

Sometimes God sends angels to carry His fame (Heb. 13:2). But more often, He simply chooses to send it through those of us who are willing to channel it.

God's fame is ready to move. He desires for it to rush through the land and meet the desperate needs of the culture. But it requires transport. And it begins with you. Are you ready to carry it?

ACKNOWLEDGMENTS

The birth of a book is a fascinating process. In the early stages, it is marked by solitude and individual toil. For me, that means countless predawn hours spent studying and writing. But even more important during this phase is what happens in my spirit as the message I am writing finds resonance with its first audience: me. Many authors write mostly from a place of experience, sharing principles they have mastered over the years. I write mostly from my current station in life and about things I desire to master, but have yet to. By and large, the concepts that make it from God's lips to the pages of a book are the ones He is currently speaking to me. They are words I am still in the process of comprehending and applying to my own life. In this way, you and I take this journey together. But those early stages of God's words refining me and beginning to make their way onto a page are spent mostly alone.

The process soon shifts dramatically, however, as the book's ability to reach readers becomes dependent on a host of others who come alongside it. From an author's perspective, it is a tremendously gratifying shift from individual toil to one of common pursuit. It is impossible for me to mention everyone who contributed to this project, but these are just a few of the giants on whose shoulders the message of this book stands.

As with so many things in my life, the core truth of this book came to me through my bride, Brooke. Habakkuk's faith-infused proclamation in Habakkuk 3:2 first pierced my heart when I saw it written in Brooke's handwriting on a chalkboard over her desk. Those twenty-six-hundred-year-old words spoken by a prophet and copied down by Brooke would not let me go. I became convinced they are words for our time. But Brooke knew it first. Thank you, baby, for your quiet faithfulness to always speak God's Word in a way that I eventually stumble into. This book simply would not be written—at least not by me—if not for you.

Jude, Brell, and Hope, it is indescribably fun to be your dad. You are at a stage where you grow and learn so very rapidly. I never cease to be inspired by your embrace of life, learning, and others. I am so glad we get to do this thing called life—and eternity—together! I am immensely proud of you. Keep your eyes on Jesus!

So much of what God is saying to me now is built on a foundation He established with those who have gone before me. For this particular project, I am especially grateful to my paternal great-grandparents, Carl and Ida Bennett, and my maternal grandparents, Owen and Ida Candler. Your collective investments will be paying spiritual dividends for all eternity. They have already literally changed my name!

While Brooke is the first person to embrace a book concept *before* me, my friend and agent Shannon Marven is the first one to hear it *from* me. Shannon, it is impossible to express the depth of my gratitude for you. It is a special gift to be able to partner with someone who sees and believes in the full picture even before I am able to fully paint it. Again, without you this book simply would not exist.

What a tremendous privilege it is to partner with Emanate Books and HarperCollins Christian Publishing on this book. There are so many who should be thanked individually, but I must single out at least a few of them. Joel Kneedler, thank you for grasping this concept so early and so fervently and for sharing the passion for getting it to the masses. You are yet another person without whom this project would not exist. Janene MacIvor, your refining touch made all the difference in the world! Thank you for your incredible attention to detail! Kristen Golden, your enthusiasm for translating this message to the marketplace is infectious. Tim Paulson, thank you for helping this project get over the line with such excellence. To everyone at Emanate Books, I am most grateful for the incredible privilege of a publishing partner willing to make decisions based first and solely on what will lift high the fame of the Famous One! It is a privilege I deeply cherish.

I would be remiss not to say a word about my pastor, Mark Batterson. My friend, you pushed me out of the starting gate on this writing journey. As grateful as I am for that push, I am even more grateful that you have continued to walk the journey with me. Thank you for believing in my writing, for lending your voice and pen to the foreword of this book, and, most importantly, for modeling such a consistent faithfulness for me as you have led our church through so many varying seasons. As I think back on the last two decades and all that God has done in and through you, I see an unflappable consistency on this point: it has always been for His fame alone. Thank you.

To you, the reader. I am grateful you chose to read this book, but as you hopefully realize by now, this is not the end of our mission, but only the beginning. The value in this book is not in what is behind you in these pages, but rather what lies before you should you choose to embrace the power of a mighty God. Are you convinced He is who He says He is? Do you see how He has intertwined His fame with yours? Will you now live only for His fame? Let's stand shoulder to shoulder together on this rampart. A mighty move of God is coming, and it is coming through you and me.

NOTES

CHAPTER 1: FAMOUS

1. Madonna Ciccone, "Madonna Quotes," Quote Authors, accessed April 2, 2019, http://www.quoteauthors.com/madonna-quotes/.
2. *Merriam-Webster, s.v. fame*, accessed April 18, 2019, https://www .merriam-webster.com/dictionary/fame.

CHAPTER 4: LOOKING OVER

1. Martin Luther King, Jr., "I've been to the Mountaintop" by Dr. Martin Luther King, Jr., AFSCME, accessed April 2, 2019, https://www.afscme.org/union/history/mlk/ive-been-to-the -mountaintop-by-dr-martin-luther-king-jr.
2. My favorite example is 2 Timothy 2:8–9, "This is my gospel, for which I am suffering even to the point of being chained like a criminal. But God's word is not chained." What a powerful example. Paul was suffering tremendously. Yet he continued to intentionally choose what would benefit the very gospel for which he was being chained.

CHAPTER 5: THE AWE FACTOR

1. Francis Chan, "The Awe Factor of God Francis Chan," YouTube video, 3:12, posted by "David C Cook," November 8, 2010, https://www.youtube.com/watch?v=LpChZxPfa-c.

NOTES

2. William Federer, *George Washington Carver: His Life and Faith in his Own Words* (St. Louis, MO, Amerisearch, 2002), 35.

CHAPTER 8: I AM WRONG
1. *Merriam-Webster, s.v. rampart*, accessed April 9, 2019, https://www.merriam-webster.com/dictionary/rampart.
2. *Merriam-Webster, s.v., parapet*, accessed April 9, 2019, https://www.merriam-webster.com/dictionary/parapet.
3. Thann Bennett. *In Search of the King* (Franklin, Worthy Publishing, 2017), xiii–xvii.

CHAPTER 9: REMEMBER TO UNDERSTAND
1. Bennett, *In Search of the King.*

CHAPTER 10: WHO KNOWS MY NAME?
1. Dotson Rader, "I Needed a Connection That Was Real," *Parade*, October 2, 2005.

CHAPTER 11: INVEST IN THE OLD MAN
1. *Merriam-Webster, s.v. persevere*, accessed April 2, 2019, https://www.merriam-webster.com/dictionary/persevere.

CHAPTER 13: DRY BONES
1. Scott Sauls, *Irresistible Faith* (Nashville, Thomas Nelson, 2019).

CHAPTER 15: MERCY ADVOCATES
1. Julie Barrier, "What Did Jesus REALLY Write in the Sand?," Crosswalk, accessed April 2, 2019, https://www.crosswalk.com/blogs/dr-julie-barrier/what-did-jesus-really-write-in-the-sand.html.

ABOUT THE AUTHOR

Thann Bennett and his wife, Brooke, live in Fort Washington, Maryland, with their three children: Jude, Gambrell, and Hope. The Bennetts are long-time members of the National Community Church family in Washington, DC. In his professional capacity, Thann is the Director of Government Affairs for the American Center for Law and Justice (ACLJ), and is a regular on-air contributor to the daily syndicated radio broadcast, *Jay Sekulow Live!* Thann is the author of *In Search of the King*, and is motivated to write by a belief that God calls those in all walks of life to draw others to a saving knowledge of Jesus Christ.